THE MINDFUL SCHOOL

# How to Teach for Transfer

Robin Fogarty
David Perkins
John Barell

Skylight Publishing
Palatine, Illinois

**The Mindful School:**
**How to Teach for Transfer**
First Printing

Published by Skylight Publishing, Inc.
200 East Wood Street, Suite 274
Palatine, Illinois 60067
1-800-348-4474 (in northern Illinois 1-708-991-6300)
FAX 1-708-991-6420

Editing: Julia E. Noblitt
Book Design: Bruce Leckie
Cover Design: David Stockman
Manuscript Entry: Donna Ramirez
Production Coordinator: Kim Overton

© 1992 by Skylight Publishing, Inc.
All Rights Reserved.

Printed in the United States of America
ISBN 0-932935-41-9

# How to Teach
# for Transfer

# TABLE OF CONTENTS

Acknowledgments / vii
Introduction / ix

## CHAPTER ONE
## "SOMETHINGS"

The "Somethings" of Transfer / 2

- Knowledge / 10
- Skills / 12
- Concepts / 14
- Attitudes / 16
- Principles / 18
- Dispositions / 20

TRANS

## CHAPTER TWO
## "SOMEHOWS"

The "Somehows" of Transfer / 26

### NEAR TRANSFER
("Hugging Strategies")

Method 1  *Setting Expectations* / 33

Method 2  *Matching* / 39

Method 3  *Simulating* / 45

Method 4  *Modeling* / 51

Method 5  *Problem-based Learning* / 57

# TABLE OF CONTENTS

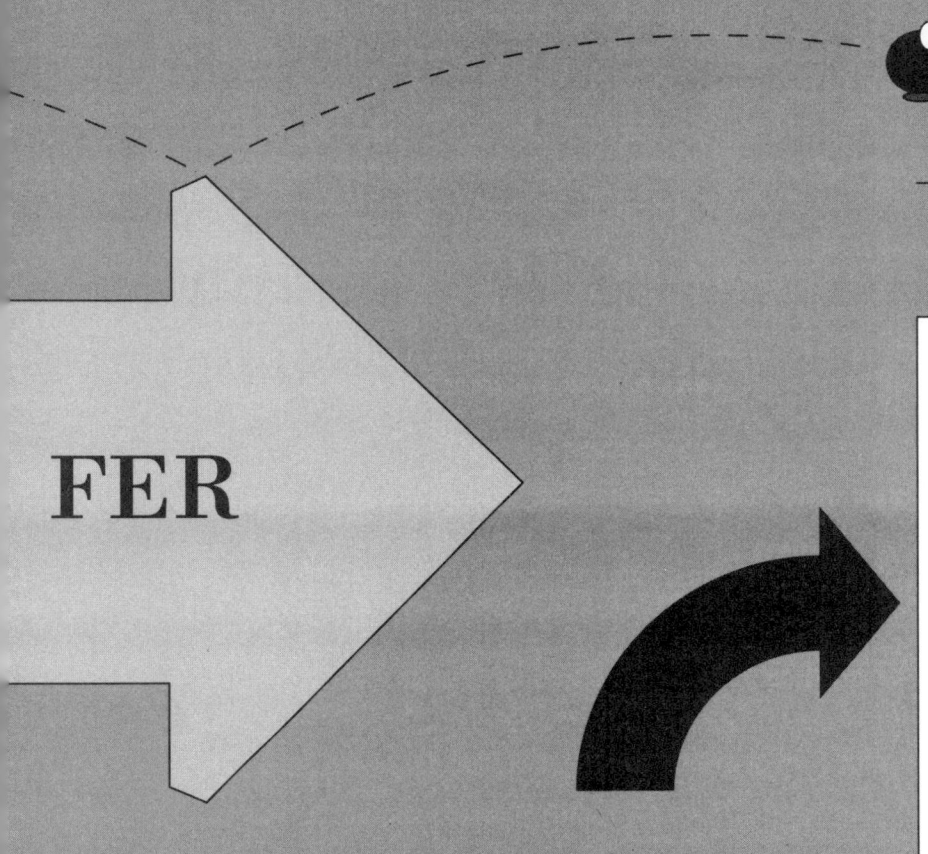

## FER

## CHAPTER THREE
## "SOMEWHERES"

The "Somewheres" of Transfer / 96

Assessing Transfer / 102

- ◆ Overlooking / 106
- ◆ Duplicating / 108
- ◆ Replicating / 110
- ◆ Integrating / 112
- ◆ Mapping / 114
- ◆ Innovating / 116

Mediating Transfer / 63

## FAR TRANSFER
("Bridging Strategies")

Method 6  *Anticipating Applications* / 67

Method 7  *Generalizing Concepts* / 73

Method 8  *Using Analogies* / 79

Method 9  *Parallel Problem Solving* / 85

Method 10  *Metacognitive Reflection* / 91

Glossary / 121
Bibliography / 129

# Acknowledgments

This model of teaching for transfer evolved over the last three years as your authors, a trio of thinking skills veterans, sought to take the thinking skills movement into a new dimension—transfer.

In our first attempt at a model in Chicago, our IRI training in the summer of 1989, we worked with fellow thinking skills advocates who were looking for extensions to their understandings about teaching thinking. While we had an embryonic form of our *something—somehow—somewhere* model, our first focus became "finding the somethings" worth transferring. We thank those pioneers for their patience and enthusiasm as we launched our earliest conception.

The following fall, working at Tempe Union High School in Tempe, Arizona, we refined the *somehows* by delineating specific mediation strategies to foster the transfer of *somethings* worth teaching. For this advance, we thank Marge Metcalf and her colleagues, who energetically embraced these techniques.

In the summer of 1990, the three of us had two distinct opportunities to further develop and refine the model for transfer. At IRI's National Training Institute in Lake Tahoe, California, we met with an eclectic group of trainers and educators from all over the country. In this supportive gathering, we defined, refined, and redefined the "language of transfer." We emerged from that experience with a deepened mutual understanding of our model. We thank these learners for their persistent questioning and rigorous inquiry that inspired us to move our model toward greater clarity and precision.

## ◆ ACKNOWLEDGMENTS ◆

By mid July 1990, in Richmond, British Columbia, freshly armed with a clearer framework, we explored the final stage of the model: targeting the *somewheres* of transfer; calling for transfer *within* the same content, *across* disciplines, and *into* life situations. We even created a superhero, "Captain Transfer" and a supervillain, "Sergeant Slug" (enthusiastically played by two of your authors) to dramatize the quest for better transfer in education. This group helped us fill in some gaps in our own thinking about the model, and proved to be lively and thoughtful participants and hosts. For this, we thank Darlene Macklam and her colleagues.

A further development in the model has emerged in the writing of this book: the tracking and assessment of transfer. As we shaped the book from our workshop experiences, the transfer continuum that helps track the transfer—the cues that tell us if the *somethings somehow* went *somewhere*—took on new meaning. This technique for monitoring transfer became the final section of the book in which we explore the *somewheres* further. For this final phase, we thank those who worked directly with the publication process—Bruce Leckie for his imaginative designs, Donna Ramirez for her "flying fingers" on the keyboard, Julie Noblitt for her editor's eye, David Stockman for his talented artwork, and Kim Overton for her ability to bring all the pieces together. We also thank the Spencer Foundation and the MacArthur Foundation, whose support of the work of David Perkins and his colleagues at Project Zero of the Harvard Graduate School of Education made possible the development of some of the ideas about transfer and thinking here translated into practice. Without the continued interest of dedicated colleagues helping us look for better ways to help children learn, we might have flagged in our efforts. So, to all who traveled with us on this journey, we express our grateful appreciation for going the distance with us.

Robin Fogarty
David Perkins
John Barell

# Introduction

## THE WHAT AND WHY OF TRANSFER

### What is Transfer?

Transfer means learning something in one context and applying it in another. For example:

- You learn to drive a car (that's the first context). Then, for a move, you rent a small truck and find that you can manage to drive the truck fairly well (that's the second context).

- You learn some strategic reading skills in English class (that's the first context). Then, later, you use the same skills in social studies (the second context).

- You learn a foreign language, say French (the first context). Later, you study Italian and find that you can carry over some particular vocabulary *and* some of the general ideas about mastering a language (so learning Italian is the second context).

- You learn how to manage squabbles better by sorting through years of fighting with a sibling (the first context). Later in life, you find the same skills useful in managing social relations on the job (the second context).

Ordinary learning contrasts with transfer. In ordinary learning, we just do more of the same thing in the same situation. To use the above examples, we drive the car some more. We use the reading strategy some more in English class. We speak French some more in French class. We squabble with our siblings less.

# ◆ INTRODUCTION ◆

Of course, any situation is a *little* different. Today's squabble with a sibling is not exactly like yesterday's. In that sense, any learning involves a little transfer. But not an interesting amount. Real transfer happens when people carry over something they learned in one context to a "significantly different" context.

## Why is Transfer Important in Education?

We need plenty of transfer for education to have the impact we want. For instance, why do we teach reading? So that students can continue to read in English class only? Certainly not. So that they deploy those skills—and *want* to deploy them—in different subject matters, and out in the world, reading newspapers, novels, job application forms, repair manuals, whatever people need to read. These are importantly different contexts. Various subject matters have their own reading demands. Think how different a story, an essay on a period in history, and a section in a math book explaining a concept are. And, outside of school, newspapers, stories, and other forms of text also have their idiosyncrasies.

Or consider mathematics. Here again, we want students to *use* their mathematical knowledge in other contexts—physics class, the supermarket, home carpentry, engineering professions. Or consider history. We want students to think historically not just in history class, but in studying literature, so that they see stories, novels, and poetry with an historical perspective; and in thinking about current events, so that they understand better the events unfolding in today's newspapers.

Basically, education that does not achieve considerable transfer is not worth much! Students may be playing the school game class-by-class. But, without transfer, they are not taking much out of each class that will serve them well anywhere else.

## Why Worry about Transfer in Education?

Some important things take care of themselves. For example, breathing is important but it takes care of itself unless you have special medical problems. Unfortunately, transfer does not take care of itself. Research shows that often students do not spontaneously transfer what we would like them to. Students do not use the mathematics from math class in physics class, the supermarket, home carpentry, or even engineering. Teachers of physics or engineering often say that students have to re-learn their math in those subjects. Students often do not use good reading strategies they have learned in English in other settings. And so on.

Even within a subject matter, transfer is important and often insufficient. Considerable research shows that a startling amount of the knowledge that people acquire in subject matter instruction is "inert." This means that the knowledge is "there" in memory for the multiple-choice quiz, but it is passive. Students do not recall it in contexts of active problem-solving, such as writing an essay. This is a problem of transfer.

The moral is that if we want transfer in education, we have to teach for transfer. Otherwise, we are not going to get nearly as much transfer as we want. It's as simple as that. And as complicated!

## KEY IDEAS ABOUT TRANSFER

The pages of this book pay repeated attention to three key ideas—the *somethings*, *somehows*, and *somewheres* of transfer. Here we will preview these ideas. But first, it's worth beginning with an even larger idea, what might be called the "spirit" of transfer.

The spirit of transfer is beautifully captured by this passage from Oliver Wendell Holmes, who writes of "the three-story intellect."

> There are one-story intellects,
> two-story intellects,
> and three-story intellects with skylights.
> All fact collectors who have
> no aim beyond their facts
> are one-story men.
> Two-story men compare, reason,
> generalize, using the labor of
> fact collectors as their own.
> Three-story men idealize,
> imagine, predict—
> their best illumination comes
> from above the skylight.
> —Oliver Wendell Holmes

Although Oliver Wendell Holmes did not write his passage specifically about transfer—and probably never heard of this slightly technical concept from the psychology of learning—certainly his notion of the three-story intellect expresses our aspirations for transfer. Mere fact collectors are not transferring at all. Those who compare, reason, generalize, are going further. And those who idealize, imagine, predict are truly reaching out.

## ◆ INTRODUCTION ◆

## Finding the "Somethings" of Transfer

*If it's not worth teaching, it's not worth teaching well.*—Eisner

The *somethings* of transfer are those things, such as math skills, reading skills, vocabulary, and historical knowledge, that students can transfer to other areas.

Armed with the critical question, "Why am I teaching this?" you are encouraged to make thoughtful decisions about what you spend your time teaching. Ask yourself, "Does it have transfer potential? How can students use it in other situations?" Arthur Costa suggests we "selectively abandon" those things without transfer potential, and "judiciously include" those things that have transfer power.

## Learning the "Somehows" of Transfer

*'There is no easy road,' Seneca wrote, 'from earth to the stars; no road, that is, except the human mind.'*—Norman Cousins

After exploring what's worth teaching for transfer, we confront the next natural question: *How* do you teach for transfer? Of course, most teachers already teach for transfer intuitively in some ways. They take opportunities to help students to make connections. But this is not the same as a systematic and persistent approach to teaching for transfer.

We devote chapter two to the *somehows* of transfer. The first part talks about "hugging" strategies for teaching for transfer. The basic idea of "hugging" is simple; you make your instruction more like the contexts to which you want transfer. That is, you "hug close to" those contexts. You can do this by setting students' expectations for transfer, simulating situations realistically, modeling so that students see what applications are like, and in other ways. The transfer that then occurs is fairly automatic for students, built into the learning experience.

The second part of chapter two focuses on "bridging" strategies. "Bridging" means helping students make connections that require them to reflect—very much like Oliver Wendell Holmes' third story. You can do this by introducing analogies and helping students to think them through, getting them to reflect metacognitively on their own thinking, and in other ways. The transfer that occurs is aware and thoughtful.

## ◆ INTRODUCTION ◆

### Targeting the "Somewheres" of Transfer

*Our mission as educators is to help every child become a more active, engaged, committed, and skillful learner, not just for a test, but for a lifetime.*—James Bellanca

The *somewheres* of transfer are the contexts we transfer *to*. Of course, in talking about the *somethings* and *somehows* of transfer, we already have been reflecting to a degree on those *somewheres*. But in the chapter focused on *somewheres* we think more closely and more systematically about them.

To target the *somewheres*, you as a teacher have to think about how the *somethings* might transfer fruitfully *within* the original content area, *across* to other disciplinary areas, and *into* life situations. Also, after targeting the *somewheres* you can seek evidence that transfer actually is occurring! There are many degrees of transfer, from students duplicating what they're taught (which is learning in the narrowest sense) to students innovating flexibly in their application of what they have learned (that third story of Oliver Wendell Holmes again).

By becoming aware of transfer, finding the *somethings*, using the *somehows*, and targeting and tracking the *somewheres*, you can make transfer a lot more likely to happen. Teaching for transfer is teaching for a lifetime!

## WHAT IS TRANSFER? SYNONYMS AND DEFINITIONS

### Definitions of Transfer

RANDOM HOUSE DICTIONARY: To convey or remove from one place, person, etc., to another.

HUNTER: The ability to learn in one situation and then to use the learning in another situation where it is appropriate; linking old learning to the new.

PERKINS: "Transfer of learning" simply means the use in a new context of knowledge and skills acquired in an earlier context. The knowledge or skill transferred can be very specific—a fact about history or grammar. Or it can be very general—a theory, a principle, a thinking skill.

**ROUGH SYNONYMS FOR TRANSFER**
(Perkins, Beyer, Sternberg, Fogarty)

Application

Use

Generalization

Extrapolation

Elaboration

Connection

# ♦ INTRODUCTION ♦

## Kinds of Transfer

There are different kinds of transfer. For our purposes here, three contrasts are worth noting: near versus far transfer, positive versus negative transfer, and low road versus high road transfer.

**Near versus far transfer.** When a student applies a writing strategy learned last week in English class to the essay assignment in the next English unit, this is near transfer. The student transfers the strategy to a rather similar situation in the same context. Now suppose the student applies the strategy in writing a constitution for the Dungeons and Dragons after-school club the student belongs to. This is far transfer—transfer to a rather different situation and setting. Of course, "near" and "far" are crude terms for the many degrees and kinds of difference that can separate situations. But the rough distinction is useful.

**Positive versus negative transfer.** Transfer is not always positive. For instance, when you vacation in England and rent a car, your right-side-of-the-road driving habits tend to transfer. Unfortunately, the English drive on the left. You have to be on the alert to prevent this negative transfer. Negative transfer often happens automatically, but rarely does mischief for long, because people quickly learn what works for them and what does not. Of course, in teaching for transfer, we aim to foster positive transfer.

**Low road versus high road transfer.** As Perkins and Salomon (1988) have written (see also Salomon and Perkins, 1989), transfer happens in two rather different ways. "Low road" transfer occurs when similarities between a new situation and an old one "trigger" the application of old knowledge and skills. "High road" transfer occurs when a person mindfully abstracts characteristics from an old situation and applies them to a new one, a reflective rather than a reflexive process. Both are important mechanisms and both can be put to good use in teaching for transfer, as we will see.

## WHEN DOES TRANSFER HAPPEN?—THE BO PEEP, LOST SHEEP, AND GOOD SHEPHERD THEORIES OF TRANSFER

We mentioned earlier that educators have good reason to worry about transfer. Research shows that often students do not transfer the knowledge and skills we would like them to. Dominant views of how readily transfer can be attained have varied over time and among different groups.

### Bo Peep Theory of Transfer: *Transfer Takes Care of Itself*

The tacit theory behind most educational practice is that transfer takes care of itself. Students learn knowledge and skills in one context and automatically transfer what they

## ◆ INTRODUCTION ◆

learn to other appropriate contexts. One might call this the "Bo Peep" theory. "Leave them alone and they'll come home wagging their tails behind them." Teach the content, give students practice that is both immediate and spaced over time, and the transfer of learning is sure to follow.

For example, we teach students the Periodic Table of Elements and give them practice in recognizing and analyzing the atomic structure of the elements. And we presume that this factual information somehow transfers into relevant application. With sufficient and varied practiced, this may actually occur. But often it will not. We also hope that students who learn the Periodic Table of Elements will somehow transfer concepts about patterns, symbolic notation, and charting information by simply working with the actual table in fact-oriented tasks. But such transfer commonly fails. Bo Peep has lost her sheep here.

## Lost Sheep Theory of Transfer: *Transfer Doesn't Happen*

Discouraged by the track record of spontaneous transfer, some theorists have concluded that people simply do not transfer very well. Knowledge and skills acquired in one context do not apply fruitfully to other contexts. By and large, learners have to learn anew in each distinctive context.

How did this view arise? At the turn of the century, it was educational dogma that Latin, geometry, and the like train the mind. However, in the early 1900s Thorndike and others presented convincing evidence that suggested that "training the faculties" indeed did not transfer in generalized ways. These researchers favored schooling in which the initial learning situation simulated as closely as possible the anticipated transfer situation.

More recently, a number of researchers have sought transfer in various situations. They have asked whether students who learn to solve one kind of problem can readily solve another with the same structure but a very different "story line" that masks the structural parallels. They have asked whether students readily apply problem-solving strategies they learn in one mathematical context to another mathematical context.

Most often (but not always) the answers were negative. Transfer did not occur (Perkins and Salomon, 1988; Salomon and Perkins, 1989). The preponderance of negative findings, as well as other developments in psychology, encouraged the idea that learning was inherently context specific. Transfer was the lost sheep of learning.

## Good Shepherd Theory of Transfer: *Transfer Will Happen with Mediation*

A number of voices from the thinking skills movement and other contexts have called for another more careful look at transfer. It's been pointed out that, while many findings

◆ INTRODUCTION ◆

reveal no transfer, a few findings show good transfer. What makes the difference? The pattern seems to be this. When the instruction includes characteristics that favor transfer, transfer occurs. Unfortunately, most instruction tends to exclude such characteristics.

What are these characteristics? According to researchers David Perkins and Gavriel Salomon (Perkins and Salomon, 1988; Salomon and Perkins, 1989), spontaneous reflexive transfer occurs only after learners have had considerable practice to "automatize" the knowledge and skills in question, and only to situations perceptually similar to the learning situation. In many learning situations, students do not receive enough practice to "automatize." And the learning situations do not often resemble the target situations to which one wants to transfer.

More thoughtful deliberate transfer tends not to occur unless the learning experience encourages students to be thoughtful—to seek generalizations, to look for opportunities to apply prior knowledge, to monitor their thinking, and ponder their strategies for approaching problems and tasks. Unfortunately, most instruction does not highlight this thoughtful side of learning.

The bottom line is that we can obtain considerable near and far transfer if we teach in ways that foster transfer. Teaching in such ways might be called "shepherding transfer," because teachers act as guides and prompters to "shepherd" knowledge and skills from one context to another. With the good shepherd theory comes a new hope for transfer. And with that new hope, of course, comes a new responsibility toward teaching for transfer—for after all, isn't all learning for transfer?

Perkins and Salomon (1988) introduced two broad mediation strategies for transfer that they call "hugging" and "bridging." "Hugging" serves reflexive transfer, the automatic kind. As mentioned earlier, "hugging" involves making the learning experience like the situations to which one wants transfer. "Bridging" serves reflective transfer. Bridging means helping students to make generalizations, monitor their thinking, and be thoughtful in other ways that foster mindful connection-making.

Beyer (1987) refers to mediation as cuing what to do, when to do it, and how to do it. His cues take the content lesson's thinking skill into new contexts. Perkins (1986) further suggests that anticipatory and retrieval tactics promote transfer (see Figure 1).

## ◆ INTRODUCTION ◆

**TRANSFER TACTICS**

|  | Anticipatory | Retrieval |
|---|---|---|
| High road | • abstracting rules<br>• anticipating applications | • reflect by generalizing the problem<br>• focus retrieval on promising prior contexts<br>• make metaphors |
| Low road | • immediate practice<br>• varied practice<br>• matching lesson to target outcome | • spaced, varied practice over time |

[Adapted from Perkins (1986)]

**Figure 1 Transfer Tactics**

# WHAT WE CAN DO ABOUT TRANSFER: A WORKING MODEL

In our work with teachers in this area of teaching for transfer, we have found a simple framework to be helpful (Perkins, Barell, and Fogarty, 1989). As we explore questions such as, "Why am I teaching this?" "Where is the transfer?" "What will the students take away from this lesson?" with teachers, we introduce this notion:

> There are *SOMETHINGS* that we *SOMEHOW*
> want to transfer *SOMEWHERE!*

To clarify this somewhat esoteric statement of transfer, we offer the diagram in Figure 2 to illustrate the *somethings, somehows,* and *somewheres* inherent in the transfer of learning.

The diagram illustrates that there are *somethings* that we want to transfer. These include the more obvious things such as curricular studies, knowledge, and skills as well as the more universal things such as principles, concepts, attitudes, and dispositions. As we plan lessons, the identified *somethings* determine the shape of those lessons. For example, if a targeted *something* is the attitude of cooperation and teamwork, the lesson will need activity components that require collaboration.

Paralleling this attention to the *somethings* of the lesson are the *somewheres*. Exactly where might this *something* transfer to? Within the content? Across to other subject matters? Or into life situations beyond the walls of the school? Determining the *somewheres* ahead of time, or anticipating future applications, also has an impact on the shape of the lesson.

### ◆ INTRODUCTION ◆

**Teaching for Transfer**

| SOMETHINGS | SOMEHOWS | SOMEWHERES |
|---|---|---|
| Knowledge | **Hugging – Low Road** | Within Content |
| Skills | Setting Expectations, Modeling, Matching, Problem-based Learning, Simulating | |
| Concepts | *Near Transfer* | |
| Attitudes | | Across Disciplines |
| Principles | **Bridging – High Road** | |
| Dispositions | Anticipating Applications, Parallel Problem Solving, Generalizing Concepts, Metacognitive Reflection, Using Analogies | Into Life |
| Criteria | *Far Transfer* | |

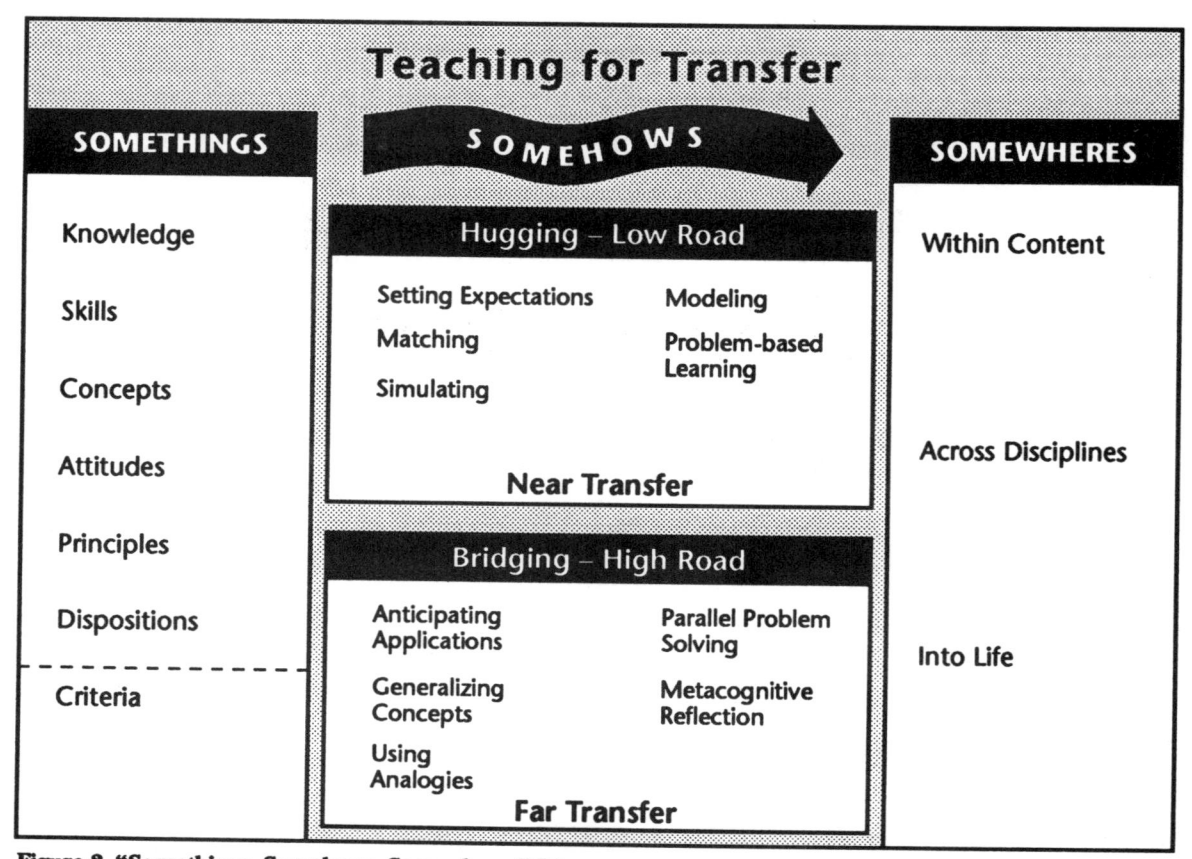

**Figure 2** "Somethings, Somehows, Somewheres" Diagram

Once the *somethings* are sifted out and the *somewheres* consciously targeted, the *somehows* of transfer become the next consideration. The center of the diagram in Figure 2 presents the *somehows*—the ways of achieving transfer discussed in this book.

These options include both low road mediation strategies that hug the transfer targets closely and high road bridging techniques that require thoughtful abstraction and application. Either way, through simple hugging strategies of setting expectations, matching, simulating, modeling, or problem-based learning or through more complex bridging strategies such as anticipating applications, generalizing concepts, using analogies, parallel problem solving, and metacognitive reflection, explicit mediation fosters the transfer of learning.

The primary focus of this book is to describe and illustrate the practical aspects of how to teach for transfer. Therefore, the emphasis is on the *somehows* or mediation strategies of transfer. However, in order to present a truly practical model of teaching for transfer, some attention must be given to ways of finding the *somethings* worth teaching and ways to target the *somewheres*.

# The Somethings, Somehows, and Somewheres of Transfer

◆

**thought unit generalis** (thôt yoo´ nit jən´ ər al´ is)
any attitude, concept, skill, principle, disposition,
or knowledge worth knowing and thinking about

# The "Somethings" of Transfer

*If it's not worth teaching, it's not worth teaching well.*—Eisner

## FINDING THE "SOMETHINGS" TO TRANSFER

At the beginning of a lesson introducing the Periodic Table of Elements, the teacher helps students look for the "somethings" worth teaching to make explicit the relevance to students for later transfer.

PHYSICS TEACHER: (Pointing to a dilapidated and yellowed Periodic Table of Elements hanging above the black lab table. The chart is framed along the bottom with an uneven fringe of frayed threads.) You will be responsible for knowing the contents of this table. It will serve you well as you work in this lab.

TIM: (with eyes rolling up...thinking to himself... I'm never gonna use this stuff ever again. What a waste. How am I ever gonna memorize all this?)

PHYSICS TEACHER: Some of you are probably thinking, "When am I ever gonna use this?"

TIM: (Sitting up with a twinge of curiosity, he waits for the punch line.)

PHYSICS TEACHER: Well, for those of you who are planning a career in the sciences, it's quite clear that the scientific knowledge contained in the chart will be invaluable to you.

# CHAPTER 1

But what about those of you who already feel that the sciences will not be a life pursuit? Let's talk a little about how learning this table might benefit you in other ways. Let's look at what might transfer for you besides the science content. Any ideas?

RENEE: I was thinking that maybe the chart itself might serve as a model for gathering information. Grids and matrices are useful tools to organize data. I use them in social studies a lot.

PHYSICS TEACHER: That's pretty insightful. How many of you have used a matrix to sort or depict information? (Three hands go up.) What else?

JOSE: The symbols on the chart remind me of Greek letters and other symbols we use in math. So I guess the idea of decoding symbolic language may be useful in other situations.

PHYSICS TEACHER: Quite so! I agree with you. The use of symbols is something we encounter throughout life. Just look at the international road signs. What else?

ROSA: Probably because I'm so involved in art, but I think the thing that is most interesting is the pattern in the chart. There are patterns in everything and these patterns help me understand—and remember things.

TIM: (Now more interested.) Yeah—and I've been thinking, too. Just figuring out how these elements are related to each other might help me see connections in other sciences.

PHYSICS TEACHER: I'm amazed at your ingenuity. Great thinking, today—Now, do we agree at least mildly, that this Period Table of Elements is worth our thinking about for a few days?

◆ SOMETHINGS ◆

# TARGETING THE SOMETHINGS

The physics class scenario illustrates how sorting out the *somethings* that are worth teaching is a crucial first step in teaching for transfer. In fact, there are three distinct reasons why teachers need to take the time to target the *somethings*. First, as never-ending curriculum demands burden already overloaded schedules, teachers find it more and more necessary to sift out the real meat of the curriculum and set curricular priorities. Second, the trend toward more holistic curriculum models of instruction also dictates the need to scrutinize the curriculum for integrating threads. And finally, as illustrated in the scenario, pulling out of the curriculum the pieces that have real "transfer power" helps students to see the relevance.

We can only teach so much. Our time and resources are limited. Yet, we want our students to learn in natural and holistic ways. And of course, we expect them to transfer that learning with ease and frequency. To uncover the sources within our curriculum that provide fertile ground for relevant student transfer, Arthur Costa (1991a) says we must "selectively abandon" and "judiciously include" curricular components. It is the work of the skilled teacher to find the *somethings* worth teaching. To become good at searching out the *somethings*, use a general framework such as the one illustrated in Figure 3. Knowledge is listed first because a knowledge base provides the critical elements for concept development. Grounded with facts, data, and information, students can begin to make vital connections that build conceptual learning.

However, isolated facts and discrete data are simply a means to an end. For example, knowledge-level facts such as "Columbus sailed in 1492" have less transfer potential than exploration (concept); "exploration often leads to discoveries that change our culture" (principle); how to plan an expedition (skill); being open to alternative possibilities (disposition/attitude). While discrete knowledge transfers for use in other subjects, knowledge that is connected to more encompassing concepts seems to have more transfer potential.

The framework in Figure 3 acts as a guide to look for particular knowledge, skills, concepts, attitudes, principles, and dispositions to emphasize in the lesson for deliberate transfer later. Each of these should be examined for transfer potential. Sifting the content through this framework reveals the real curricular priorities as the teacher weighs the results against the district philosophy, academic criterion, and student relevance.

◆ SOMETHINGS ◆

---

**Somethings:** _____
                                      lesson/unit/topic

**KNOWLEDGE:** facts, data, statistics, and information (dates, events, equations)

**SKILLS:** routines, procedures (e.g., cooperation, prediction, outlining)

**CONCEPTS:** domain-specific or universal; "big ideas"; umbrella themes (e.g., photosynthesis, courage)

**ATTITUDES:** feelings, profiles, tone, emotions (e.g., kind, courageous, reserved, jealous)

**PRINCIPLES:** rules, laws, theorems, heuristics (e.g., 2nd Law of Thermodynamics; Pythagorean Theorem)

**DISPOSITIONS:** behaviors, habits, postures, tendencies (e.g., impulsiveness, sense of humor)

---

**Figure 3 Somethings Framework**

## Criteria for Worthwhile Topics

What makes a topic worthwhile as a candidate for transfer is, of course, its potential significance in other areas. In appraising a topic's potential, one can check the following three areas:

- *Significance within the disciplines*—does the topic have broad significance within its own and perhaps other disciplines?

- *Societal significance*—does the topic speak to problems and concerns of society at large?

- *Student needs/interests/aspirations*—does the topic resonate with students' hopes, desires, curiosities, needs, and so on?

For example, if we are studying human digestion, what are the concepts, ideas, and principles needed to understand this system? As the teacher examines the unit on the digestive system, a completed framework might look like the one in Figure 4. Note the memos on the side of the chart that show the teacher's reflective thoughts about how to approach this unit and get the most transfer power from it.

This process of searching for the *somethings* worth teaching can be done quite painlessly after a few rounds of practice. Of course, many of us already carry out this sort of analysis casually in our heads as we look to upcoming units. But, the process of setting curriculum priorities should become a deliberate and systematic procedure to make the most of transfer opportunities. Including students in the discussion and planning process is one good strategy. Such strategies work well in inquiry units where we disclose the significant concepts and ideas with questions such as "What do you already know?" and "What do you want to find out?"

Once we begin this conversation about "What's worth teaching?" and "What's worth thinking about for a longer period of time?" and "Where is the transfer power in this content?", we can use it to examine past units of study as well. Sometimes it's easier to look back at a lesson or unit just completed and sift out the priority pieces for the next time you teach it. Sometimes it's easier to work through the priorities in professional dialogue with colleagues. As a pre-planning strategy or as an evaluation tool, setting curricular priorities—finding the "somethings worth teaching"—must guide instruction in our schools.

◆ S O M E T H I N G S ◆

## "SOMETHINGS": *Digestive System*
lesson/unit/topic

| FIRST PASS... | SECOND THOUGHTS... |
|---|---|
| Digestive System Search for "somethings" | Maybe I should expand the topic to "Systems in the Body" or "Your Inner Environment" |
| **KNOWLEDGE:** human anatomy vocabulary, digestive system per se | The text is the best resource here, but will need some library time. |
| **SKILLS:** diagramming, flow charts, use of analogies | I need to target one major thinking skill—maybe sequencing; can use graphic organizers to illustrate and utilize skill. Using analogies is a possible way to culminate unit. |
| **CONCEPTS:** systems, loops, assimilation | "Systems" is the universal concept but I like the idea of "inner environment"—then I could do health, nutrition, substance abuse prevention, and self-esteem—fertile. |
| **ATTITUDE:** value good health, nutritious diet | This would fit with the expanded concept idea. |
| **PRINCIPLES:** cause/effect relationship | Cause and effect could also be the thinking skill focus; more sophisticated than sequencing. |
| **DISPOSITIONS:** Self-awareness of bodily functions. Whole health and fitness point of view. | Like the idea of connecting this to health/fitness focus. |

### "SOMETHINGS" WITH TRANSFER POWER

- Inner environment or systems
- Determining cause/effect relationships
- Self-Esteem

NOTE: Use graphic organizers, flow chart, cause-effect circles, decision tree.

**Figure 4 Sample Somethings Framework**

The Somethings of Transfer

♦ INSPIRATIONS ♦

◆ SOMETHINGS ◆

# Reflect on the "Somethings" of Transfer

◆ S O M E T H I N G S ◆

# Knowledge
A Sample

*THINK ABOUT*...a lesson, unit, topic, chapter, or theme. List all the **facts, data, statistics,** and **information** that could be targets for transfer of knowledge within and across content areas and into life situations. Include: vocabulary words, definitions, equations, dates, and other input that make up the needed knowledge base.

**Design a lesson with the relevant knowledge elements**

Focus:  Science          Circulatory Unit

vocabulary:  veins          identify:  radial
             arteries                  ulnar
             heart                     renal
             valves                    vena cava
             jugular

HOW TO TEACH FOR TRANSFER

◆ S O M E T H I N G S ◆

# Knowledge
## Your Example

***THINK ABOUT***...a lesson, unit, topic, chapter, or theme. List all the **facts, data, statistics,** and **information** that could be targets for transfer of knowledge within and across content areas and into life situations. Include: vocabulary words, definitions, equations, dates, and other input that make up the needed knowledge base.

**Design a lesson with the relevant knowledge elements**

*Focus:*

◆ S O M E T H I N G S ◆

# Skills
## A Sample

***THINK ABOUT***...a lesson, unit, topic, chapter, or theme. List all the **skills, routines,** and **procedures** that could be targets for transfer of knowledge within and across content areas and into life situations. Include: thinking skills (prediction), skills of cooperation (listening), conflict management (consensus), research and organizational skills (memoing), memory and study skills (test-taking), as well as practical content skills such as keyboarding and operating equipment.

**Design a lesson with the relevant knowledge elements**

Focus: Reading            Paragraphing
Finding the main idea/paragraph
Formations/Text organizers (e.g., there are three... First, Second, Finally)

# Skills
Your Example

***THINK ABOUT...*** a lesson, unit, topic, chapter, or theme. List all the **skills, routines,** and **procedures** that could be targets for transfer of knowledge within and across content areas and into life situations. Include: thinking skills (prediction), skills of cooperation (listening), conflict management (consensus), research and organizational skills (memoing), memory and study skills (test-taking), as well as practical content skills such as keyboarding and operating equipment.

**Design a lesson with the relevant knowledge elements**

*Focus:*

◆ S O M E T H I N G S ◆

# Concepts
## A Sample

***THINK ABOUT***...a lesson, unit, topic, chapter, or theme. List all the **concepts (domain-specific or universal)**, **"big ideas,"** and **umbrella themes** that could be targets for transfer within and across content areas and into life situations. Include: concepts such as cycles, patterns, or conflict as well as "big ideas" such as attributes of an era or a class. Search for generalizations that students could take away and use in other situations.

**Design a lesson with the relevant knowledge elements**

Focus:   *Global Studies*          *Exploration*
         *Conflict/Disputes*
         *War/Aggression*

◆ S O M E T H I N G S ◆

# Concepts
## Your Example

***THINK ABOUT*...** a lesson, unit, topic, chapter, or theme. List all the **concepts (domain-specific or universal),** **"big ideas,"** and **umbrella themes** that could be targets for transfer within and across content areas and into life situations. Include: concepts such as cycles, patterns, or conflict as well as "big ideas" such as attributes of an era or a class. Search for generalizations that students could take away and use in other situations.

**Design a lesson with the relevant knowledge elements**

*Focus:*

◆ S O M E T H I N G S ◆

# Attitudes
## A Sample

***THINK ABOUT***...a lesson, unit, topic, chapter, or theme. List all the **attitudes, profiles, feelings, tone,** and **emotions** that could be targets for transfer within and across content areas and into life situations. Include: attitudes (kind, friendly, hostile), profiles (courageous, unremitting, submissive), tone (sarcastic, cynical, sincere), and emotions (sadness, anger, joy).

**Design a lesson with the relevant knowledge elements**

Focus: *Health      Substance Abuse Prevention*
*Efficacy/Inadequacy*

♦ S O M E T H I N G S ♦

# Attitudes
## Your Example

***THINK ABOUT***...a lesson, unit, topic, chapter, or theme. List all the **attitudes, profiles, feelings, tone,** and **emotions** that could be targets for transfer within and across content areas and into life situations. Include: attitudes (kind, friendly, hostile), profiles (courageous, unremitting, submissive), tone (sarcastic, cynical, sincere), and emotions (sadness, anger, joy).

**Design a lesson with the relevant knowledge elements**

*Focus:*

◆ S O M E T H I N G S ◆

# Principles
### A Sample

***THINK ABOUT***...a lesson, unit, topic, chapter, or theme. List all the **principles, rules, theorems, laws,** and **heuristics** that could be targets for transfer within subject matter, across disciplines, or into life situations. Include: principles (democracy, levers and pulleys, the associative principle of math), rules ("i" before "e" except after "c"), laws (the law of gravity or the second law of thermodynamics); theorems (syllogisms—if . . . then).

### Design a lesson with the relevant knowledge elements

Focus:  *Math*          *Algebra*

*Doing the same thing to both sides of an equation preserves the equality.*

HOW TO TEACH FOR TRANSFER

◆ S O M E T H I N G S ◆

# Principles
Your Example

***THINK ABOUT***...a lesson, unit, topic, chapter, or theme. List all the **principles, rules, theorems, laws,** and **heuristics** that could be targets for transfer within subject matter, across disciplines, or into life situations. Include: principles (democracy, levers and pulleys, the associative principle of math), rules ("i" before "e" except after "c"), laws (the law of gravity or the second law of thermodynamics); theorems (syllogisms—if . . . then).

**Design a lesson with the relevant knowledge elements**

*Focus:*

The Somethings of Transfer

◆ S O M E T H I N G S ◆

# Dispositions
## A Sample

***THINK ABOUT***...a lesson, unit, topic, chapter, or theme. List all the **skills**, **routines**, and **procedures** that could be targets for transfer within subject matter, across disciplines, or into life situations. Include ways to approach problems, implement solutions, and evaluate tendencies as well as generally observable traits (sense of humor, openness).

**Design a lesson with the relevant knowledge elements**

Focus:   *Physical Education (PE)*   *Gymnastics*
        *Perseverance*
        *Perfection*

◆ S O M E T H I N G S ◆

# Dispositions
## Your Example

***THINK ABOUT***...a lesson, unit, topic, chapter, or theme. List all the **skills**, **routines**, and **procedures** that could be targets for transfer within subject matter, across disciplines, or into life situations. Include ways to approach problems, implement solutions, and evaluate tendencies as well as generally observable traits (sense of humor, openness).

**Design a lesson with the relevant knowledge elements**

*Focus:*

### ◆ SOMETHINGS ◆

Use this planner to scan for the possibilities of "somethings" worth teaching for transfer.

# The Model
## Finding the "Somethings"

**Topic:** *The Circulatory System*

**Knowledge**
- elements of circulatory system
- how the circulatory system works
- cardiovascular system

**Skills**
- sequencing
- cause and effect

**Concepts**
- systems
- circuits

**Attitudes**
- appreciation of the intricacies of the human body

**Principles**
- principles of a pump

**Dispositions**
- healthy habits of cardiovascular training

**Criteria**
1. relevance to students' lives
2. life-long application
3. traditional science unit
4. high interest for students

HOW TO TEACH FOR TRANSFER

◆ S O M E T H I N G S ◆

Use this planner to scan for the possibilities of "somethings" worth teaching for transfer.

# The Model
Finding the "Somethings"

Topic:

**Knowledge**

**Skills**

**Concepts**

**Attitudes**

**Principles**

**Dispositions**

**Criteria**

The Somethings of Transfer

◆ S O M E T H I N G S ◆

# Criteria
### What's Worth Teaching?

Three possible criteria are cited here. As you consider each one, jot down your thoughts and rationale.

*Topic: Explorers*

- *Significance within the disciplines*—does the topic have broad significance within its own, and perhaps other, disciplines?

   *The topic of explorers and the concept of exploration has significance and application in many fields — e.g., space exploration; genetic engineering as an exploratory field; exploring diverse cultures; exploring solutions.*

- *Societal significance*—does the topic speak to problems and concerns of society at large?

   *The idea of ongoing exploration has societal implications for the present and the future.*

- *Student needs/interests/aspirations*—does the topic resonate with students' hopes, desires, curiosities, needs, and so on?

   *Young people are often intrigued with the concept of exploration and the adventures of the explorers.*

- *Other* criteria might include these ideas or others that you develop.

◆ S O M E T H I N G S ◆

# Criteria
### What's Worth Teaching?

Three possible criteria are cited here. As you consider each one, jot down your thoughts and rationale.

- *Significance within the disciplines*—does the topic have broad significance within its own, and perhaps other, disciplines?

- *Societal significance*—does the topic speak to problems and concerns of society at large?

- *Student needs/interests/aspirations*—does the topic resonate with students' hopes, desires, curiosities, needs, and so on?

- *Other* criteria might include these ideas or others that you develop.

# The "Somehows" of Transfer

*'There is no easy road,'
Seneca wrote, 'from earth
to the stars; no road, that
is, except the human
mind.'*

—Norman Cousins

## USING THE "SOMEHOWS" OF TRANSFER

Using the history chapter on the causes of World War II for content, the history teacher targets the skill of asking good questions as part of the lesson focus. The specific type of questioning or the "something" that is targeted is metacognitive reflection questions. This scenario illustrates how a history teacher uses a "bridging" strategy to facilitate meaningful transfer.

HISTORY TEACHER: Your assignment involves two parts. Part I: Review the questions at the back of the chapter and with a partner categorize them as either "Skinny" questions that can be answered directly from reading the text or as "Fat" questions that go beyond the given information.

MELISSA: Question? Can you give us examples?

HISTORY TEACHER: Better yet, let me pose a question. You value it, "fat" or "skinny." Here's one. What were some significant battles of World War II?

MELISSA: That seems pretty narrow. I think it's a skinny question.

# CHAPTER 2

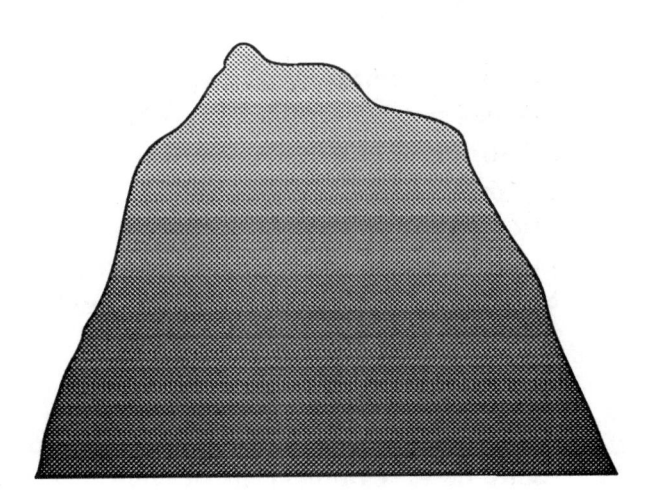

HISTORY TEACHER: How about this? Defend one of the following statements: "Great men make great events" or "Great events make great men."

MELISSA: Definitely "fat." I would have to give lots of supporting evidence—it would turn into a long answer.

HISTORY TEACHER: That's right! You've got the idea. Now, Part II of the assignment (I didn't forget!) is to select questions from your list and write your answers to turn in.

ANDREW: (hand waving in the air)

HISTORY TEACHER: Will this be a fat question or a skinny question, Andrew?

ANDREW: Skinny!

HISTORY TEACHER: O.K., what's your question?

ANDREW: How many questions should we answer?

HISTORY TEACHER: You're right, that was a skinny question! The answer is four. Write answers to two fat and two skinny questions.

## The "Somehows" of Transfer

This chapter presents practical strategies to insure that *somethings* worth transferring are taught in such a way that students internalize, apply, and transfer them appropriately. According to Perkins' and Salomon's "Good Shepherd Theory" outlined in the introduction, transfer must be "shepherded" or helped along. The *somehows* are the mediating strategies that shepherd or promote relevant transfer.

◆ S O M E H O W S ◆

There are two roads to transfer: the low road of near or simple transfer and the high road of far or complex transfer. We may design lessons that "hug" the expected outcome if we are looking for near and somewhat automatic transfer. For example, if we want students to become better writers, we have them write, rather than circle answers in a multiple choice worksheet model. In contrast, we can select "bridging" strategies that call for mindful abstractions when we want far transfer. For example, if we want students to connect the problem solving they do in math class with the problem solving they do in the scientific method, we might orchestrate a discussion that leads students to generalize about problem solving in order to bridge problem solving in math to problem solving in science. Moreover, we can map out combinations of both hugging and bridging strategies to boost transfer all the more.

For example, if we want students to read materials of all sorts more strategically, we might both (a) engage students in brainstorming different reading situations and analyzing how useful basic reading strategies like "prereading" might be in those situations (bridging) and (b) actually give students experience in applying these strategies to different kinds of materials (hugging).

## Mediating Strategies

In Figure 5, ten *somehows* are presented: five "hugging" strategies to facilitate near or simple transfer and five "bridging" strategies to span wide gaps between original learnings and remote situations (far or complex transfer).

Shepherding transfer with the selective use of these ten hugging and bridging strategies can easily become an integral part of your lesson planning. It's just a matter of consciously targeting transfer as a desired outcome, rather than assuming that transfer will happen automatically. Once transfer becomes a goal, it's easy to choose appropriate strategies.

Although these strategies for mediating transfer make up only a partial list of the "somehows," they represent explicit tools for transfer for our instructional repertoire. As we become more conscious of teaching for transfer, we will find further creative ways to facilitate transfer and continually add these instructional tools to our "teacher's tool kit."

## TEACHING FOR TRANSFER MEDIATION STRATEGIES

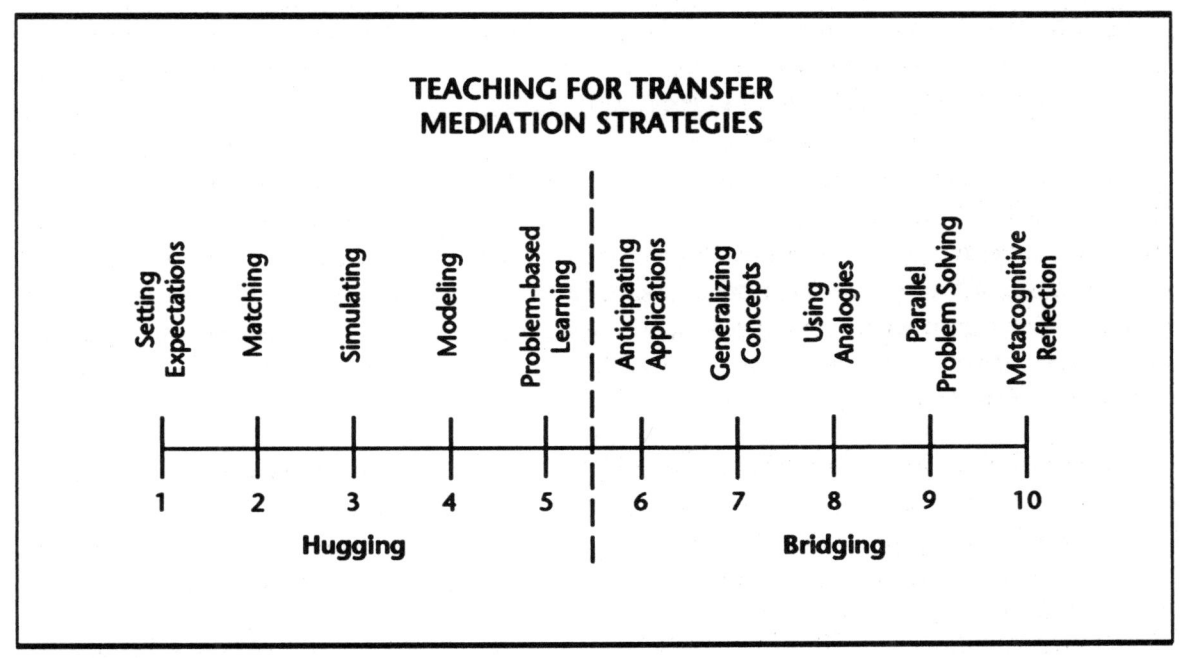

A scale from 1 to 10, divided into Hugging (1–5) and Bridging (6–10):

1. Setting Expectations
2. Matching
3. Simulating
4. Modeling
5. Problem-based Learning
6. Anticipating Applications
7. Generalizing Concepts
8. Using Analogies
9. Parallel Problem Solving
10. Metacognitive Reflection

**Figure 5 Ten Somehows**

# MEDIATING TRANSFER: HUGGING STRATEGIES

- *Setting Expectations*: Alerting learners to direct applications

- *Matching*: Experiencing, immersing

- *Simulating*: Role playing, acting out

- *Modeling*: Showing, demonstrating

- *Problem-based Learning*: Learning content through solving problems

## Near Transfer/Low Road/Hugging

NEAR TRANSFER   We draw a rough distinction between "near transfer" and "far transfer." Near transfer refers to transfer between contexts that are quite similar. Here are some examples of near transfer:

- Using a problem-solving skill you acquired in math for another kind of problem in math.

- Using a piece of historical knowledge in thinking about another episode in history, making a comparison.
- Using skills for driving a car for driving a small truck.

**LOW ROAD TRANSFER**  Low road transfer is one of two fundamental mechanisms of transfer identified by Gavriel Salomon and David Perkins. Low road transfer occurs by the automatic triggering of well-learned knowledge or skills by similar situations. It is not a very thoughtful, intellectual process, but more of a spontaneous, reflexive one. It is thus more efficient than high road transfer, but yields near transfer much more than far transfer. Low road transfer can reach somewhat further over time, because knowledge and skills can gradually spread from one context to a similar one, to another similar one, and so on. Thus, low road transfer is facilitated by practicing knowledge and skills in a variety of similar contexts, thus "spreading out" the knowledge or skills over time.

Here are some examples of low road transfer:

- A student learns basic arithmetic skills in arithmetic; these are automatically evoked when an arithmetic problem arises in science.
- Students learn a problem-solving strategy for one kind of arithmetic problem. The teacher immediately gives a somewhat different kind of problem, but with some similarity. Students carry over the strategy to the new kind of problem, thus "spreading" its utility more widely.
- The English teacher teaches some basic reading strategies, giving students practice in several different kinds of reading to "spread" the habit across multiple genres.

**HUGGING**  Hugging techniques foster transfer by making the learning contexts more like the desired contexts of application. Hugging means that the initial learning situation resembles as much as possible the anticipated application context. One of the great paradoxes of education is that we often teach for outcomes without making students' learning experiences resemble very much the outcomes we hope for. For example, we teach history in the hope that students will gain a better perspective on the modern world, but often current events are never brought into history class and compared with the history under study. We teach arithmetic in hopes that learners will use it in the supermarket and other practical contexts, but often do little to simulate in the classroom what such uses would be like. Hugging—making the learning context more like the application context—relies on the mechanism of low road transfer.

◆ S O M E H O W S ◆

# Near Transfer

## "Hugging"

## ◆ INSPIRATIONS ◆

## ◆ SOMEHOWS ◆

### HUGGING

# Setting Expectations
### "Alerting Learners to Direct Applications"

**Method 1**

**DEFINITION**—talking to students about expectations for near transfer to increase the likelihood that transfer will happen; explicitly planning into lessons the questions or tasks that help students connect across content so transfer is more likely to occur.

This "hugs" closer to targeted near transfers by building students' awareness of them and encouraging students to apply what they are learning in a straightforward manner. Too often, we teach without awakening students to the payoffs.

### LESSON EXAMPLE
When studying the skill of detecting bias in social studies, engage students in brainstorming a list of situations where they might look for bias (TV, newspapers, playground talk, etc.) and encourage them to bring back examples.

### VERBAL CUES
- "What's the big idea?"
- "How does this connect to what you already know?"
- "Where might you use this?"
- "Do you see how this might fit in with what we were working with last week?"
- "How is this relevant?"

### METHODS
- Set the stage for future use.
- Let students know they are *supposed to* use this elsewhere.

### NEAR TRANSFER

The Somehows of Transfer

◆ S O M E H O W S ◆

## HUGGING

# Setting Expectations
### A Sample

THINK ABOUT...a lesson, unit, topic, chapter, or theme. Note some ways to **set expectations** for future use; **anticipate relevance; develop rationale** for shepherding transfer of the targeted somethings. Include ways to set expectations prior to the instruction (Why bother to learn this?), throughout the instructional unit (What does this remind you of?), and for short-term and long-term use following the teaching (How can you use this?).

Focus: *Math        Fraction Unit*

### Beginning of the Lesson

Identify somethings with transfer potential.

*Brainstorm opportunities to use fractions (e.g., 1/2 a candy bar)*

### Middle of the Lesson

Remind students of targeted somethings and how they might be used.

*Scout for "fractions" and keep a journal list.*

### End of the Lesson

Where else might we use this?

*Add to the originally brainstormed list of when we use fractions in our academic and personal lives.*

**NEAR TRANSFER**

◆ S O M E H O W S ◆

## HUGGING

# Setting Expectations
### Your Example

***THINK BACK...***to a lesson, unit, topic, chapter, or theme. Note some ways to *set expectations* for future use; *anticipate relevance;* **develop rationale** for shepherding transfer of the targeted somethings. Include ways to set expectations prior to the instruction (Why bother to learn this?), throughout the instructional unit (What does this remind you of?), and for short-term and long-term use following the teaching (How can you use this?). ***Redesign*** by setting expectations to hug for transfer.

*Focus:*

### Beginning of the Lesson
*Identify somethings with transfer potential.*

### Middle of the Lesson
*Remind students of targeted somethings and how they might be used.*

### End of the Lesson
*Where else might we use this?*

NEAR TRANSFER

The Somehows of Transfer

◆ S O M E H O W S ◆

### HUGGING

# Setting Expectations
Your Example

*THINK AHEAD*...to a lesson, unit, topic, chapter, or theme. Note some ways to *set expectations* for future use; *anticipate relevance; develop rationale* for shepherding transfer of the targeted somethings. Include ways to set expectations prior to the instruction (Why bother to learn this?), throughout the instructional unit (What does this remind you of?), and for short-term and long-term use following the teaching (How can you use this?). *Design* by setting expectations to hug for transfer.

*Focus:*

### Beginning of the Lesson

*Identify somethings with transfer potential.*

### Middle of the Lesson

*Remind students of targeted somethings and how they might be used.*

### End of the Lesson

*Where else might we use this?*

NEAR TRANSFER

## ◆ SOMEHOWS ◆

**HUGGING**

# Setting Expectations
## Your Example

***THINK AGAIN*** ...of a lesson, unit, topic, chapter, or theme. Note some ways to ***set expectations*** for future use; ***anticipate relevance; develop rationale*** for shepherding transfer of the targeted somethings. Include ways to set expectations prior to the instruction (Why bother to learn this?), throughout the instructional unit (What does this remind you of?), and for short-term and long-term use following the teaching (How can you use this?). ***Refine*** by setting expectations to hug for transfer.

*Focus:*

### Beginning of the Lesson

*Identify somethings with transfer potential.*

### Middle of the Lesson

*Remind students of targeted somethings and how they might be used.*

### End of the Lesson

*Where else might we use this?*

**NEAR TRANSFER**

The Somehows of Transfer

♦ INSPIRATIONS ♦

### ◆ SOMEHOWS ◆

**HUGGING**

# Method 2

# Matching
"Experiencing, Immersing"

**DEFINITION**—matching the lesson design to the desired outcome; engaging the student in the performance you're trying to develop; guiding the targeted behavior; using procedural learning; experiential learning; immersion.

This "hugs" by trying to make the learning experiences resemble the actual applications. Too often, we teach with exercises that do not give learners direct experience with the very skills we want them to develop.

### LESSON EXAMPLE

If the goal is to get students to take a stand, advocate a position, and support it with detail, give them many opportunities to engage in that behavior. For example, weave agree/disagree questions throughout a lecturette. Have students practice "taking a stand" as they learn the art of public advocacy; write persuasive essays; defend their critique of a painting; or debate.

### VERBAL CUES
- "Practice the model."
- "Try it."
- "Duplicate this."
- "Repeat the process."
- "Follow the steps."

### METHODS
- Create an activity to match intended outcome.
- Use experiential learning.

**NEAR TRANSFER**

The Somehows of Transfer

◆ S O M E H O W S ◆

**HUGGING**

# Matching
## A Sample

*THINK ABOUT...a lesson, unit, topic, chapter, or theme. Note some ways to engage students in the desired performance; immerse students in the expected learning; or construct an experiential design to shepherd transfer of the targeted somethings. Include: procedural guided learning tasks (step-by-step recipes); experiential hands-on approaches (manipulation or lab experiments); or immersion into the field of study (a French immersion class or an archaeological dig).*

Focus: *Language Arts*     *Paraphrasing: Topic Sentence*

### Beginning of the Lesson

*What do I want students to be able to do?*

   *Using an overhead, develop a paragraph with a topic sentence.*

### Middle of the Lesson

*Are students practicing the desired behavior?*

   *Have small groups write a paragraph with an obvious topic sentence using a text organizer and then cut sentences apart and scramble them.*

### End of the Lesson

*Can students do what I wanted them to do?*

   *Reassemble another group's sentence strips, identifying the topic sentence with text organizer and clues and the supporting sentence.*

**NEAR TRANSFER**

HOW TO TEACH FOR TRANSFER

◆ S O M E H O W S ◆

### HUGGING

# Matching
Your Example

*THINK BACK...* to a lesson, unit, topic, chapter, or theme. Note some ways to *engage students in the desired performance; immerse students in the expected learning; or construct an experiential design* to shepherd transfer of the targeted somethings. Include: procedural guided learning tasks (step-by-step recipes); experiential hands-on approaches (manipulation or lab experiments); or immersion into the field of study (a French immersion class or an archaeological dig). *Redesign* with matching to hug for the desired transfer.

*Focus:*

### Beginning of the Lesson

*What do I want students to be able to do?*

### Middle of the Lesson

*Are students practicing the desired behavior?*

### End of the Lesson

*Can students do what I wanted them to do?*

NEAR TRANSFER

The Somehows of Transfer

## HUGGING

# Matching
### Your Example

*THINK AHEAD* ...to a lesson, unit, topic, chapter, or theme. Note some ways to *engage students in the desired performance; immerse students in the expected learning; or construct an experiential design* to shepherd transfer of the targeted somethings. Include: procedural guided learning tasks (step-by-step recipes); experiential hands-on approaches (manipulation or lab experiments); or immersion into the field of study (a French immersion class or an archaeological dig). *Design* with matching to hug for the desired transfer.

*Focus:*

### Beginning of the Lesson

*What do I want students to be able to do?*

### Middle of the Lesson

*Are students practicing the desired behavior?*

### End of the Lesson

*Can students do what I wanted them to do?*

NEAR TRANSFER

## ◆ SOMEHOWS ◆

### HUGGING

# Matching
### Your Example

***THINK AGAIN***...of a lesson, unit, topic, chapter, or theme. Note some ways to *engage students in the desired performance; immerse students in the expected learning;* or *construct an experiential design* to shepherd transfer of the targeted somethings. Include: procedural guided learning tasks (step-by-step recipes); experiential hands-on approaches (manipulation or lab experiments); or immersion into the field of study (a French immersion class or an archaeological dig). *Refine* with matching to hug for the desired transfer.

*Focus:*

### Beginning the Lesson

*What do I want students to be able to do?*

### Middle of the Lesson

*Are students practicing the desired behavior?*

### End of the Lesson

*Can students do what I wanted them to do?*

### NEAR TRANSFER

The Somehows of Transfer

◆ INSPIRATIONS ◆

◆ S O M E H O W S ◆

## HUGGING

# Method 3

# Simulating
"Role Playing, Acting Out"

**DEFINITION**—role playing, personifying, or simulating the "real thing" to hug the desired outcome; experiencing the actions and feelings of the actual situation by pretending or approximating the real experience.

### LESSON EXAMPLE
In Driver Education classes, have students simulate driving before they drive an actual car. Or, act out the job interview taking on the role of the interviewee. Role play the trial of the big bad wolf (e.g., "The Three Little Pigs") to learn about bias and jury selection.

### VERBAL CUES
- "Pretend."
- "Put yourself in his or her place."
- "Imagine."
- "Take his or her role."
- "How might he or she think about this?"

### METHODS
- Simulation games
- Use simulators if available (e.g., driver's education).

NEAR TRANSFER

◆ S O M E H O W S ◆

### HUGGING

# Simulating
### A Sample

**THINK ABOUT**...a lesson, unit, topic, chapter, or theme. Note some ways to *simulate the "real thing"; to role play or act out; and to personify or pretend* in order to shepherd transfer of the targeted somethings. Include ways to simulate (setting up prototypes); role play or act out (assigning specific parts); personify or pretend (assuming actions and feelings of another).

Focus: *Career Education*          *Job Interviews*

**Beginning of the Lesson**

*How can we simulate the real thing?*

> *Predict possible questions the employer might ask.*

**Middle of the Lesson**

*How realistic is the simulation?*

> *Set up simulation of job interview with roles for employer and candidate.*

**End of the Lesson**

*How accurate has our simulation been?*

> *Try to assume the role of employer and evaluate the interview; determine how the employer saw you as a candidate.*

### NEAR TRANSFER

## ◆ SOMEHOWS ◆

### HUGGING

# Simulating
### Your Example

*THINK BACK*...to a lesson, unit, topic, chapter, or theme. Note some ways to *simulate the "real thing"; to role play or act out; and to personify or pretend* in order to shepherd transfer of the targeted somethings. Include ways to simulate (setting up prototypes); role play or act out (assigning specific parts); personify or pretend (assuming actions and feelings of another). *Redesign* for transfer of the targeted somethings.

*Focus:*

### Beginning of the Lesson

*How can we simulate the real thing?*

### Middle of the Lesson

*How realistic is the simulation?*

### End of the Lesson

*How accurate has our simulation been?*

### NEAR TRANSFER

The Somehows of Transfer

◆ SOMEHOWS ◆

### HUGGING

# Simulating
### Your Example

***THINK AHEAD***...to a lesson, unit, topic, chapter, or theme. Note some ways to ***simulate the "real thing"; to role play or act out; and to personify or pretend*** in order to shepherd transfer of the targeted somethings. Include ways to simulate (setting up prototypes); role play or act out (assigning specific parts); personify or pretend (assuming actions and feelings of another). ***Design*** for transfer of the targeted somethings.

*Focus:*

### Beginning of the Lesson

*How can we simulate the real thing?*

### Middle of the Lesson

*How realistic is the simulation?*

### End of the Lesson

*How accurate has our simulation been?*

NEAR TRANSFER

HOW TO TEACH FOR TRANSFER

### HUGGING

# Simulating
Your Example

***THINK AGAIN***...of a lesson, unit, topic, chapter, or theme. Note some ways to ***simulate the "real thing"***; ***to role play or act out***; ***and to personify or pretend*** in order to shepherd transfer of the targeted somethings. Include ways to simulate (setting up prototypes); role play or act out (assigning specific parts); personify or pretend (assuming actions and feelings of another). ***Refine*** for transfer of the targeted somethings.

*Focus:*

### Beginning of the Lesson

*How can we simulate the real thing?*

### Middle of the Lesson

*How realistic is the simulation?*

### End of the Lesson

*How accurate has our simulation been?*

### NEAR TRANSFER

◆ I N S P I R A T I O N S ◆

## ◆ S O M E H O W S ◆

### HUGGING

# Method 4

# Modeling
### "Showing, Demonstrating"

**DEFINITION**—demonstrating the desired behavior with a running monologue about what you're doing; modeling the behavior for students to adopt and talking about it by labeling the behaviors; making sense of the demonstration.

This "hugs" desired transfers because modeling is more like the target behaviors than verbal descriptions, especially verbal statements of abstract principles. Too often, we teach too abstractly, without *showing* students what we mean.

### LESSON EXAMPLE

When asking students to *prioritize* their homework assignments, the teacher will first create the list of items on the board while telling about it. For instance, "Here's how I prioritize. Once I have listed all the things I want to do, I find the *most* urgent items and rank those number 1, 2, and 3. Then I find the *least* important items; things I would like to do, but are not due the next day. I rank those toward the bottom. Then I sort out the middle items. Now I have prioritized my work."

### VERBAL CUES

- "Here's an example."
- "Let me illustrate."
- "This is a specific instance."
- "Let me show you."
- "Use this as a prototype."

### METHODS

- Demonstrate "think aloud" thought process.
- Reflect on process.

### NEAR TRANSFER

**The Somehows of Transfer**

◆ S O M E H O W S ◆

**HUGGING**

# Modeling
## A Sample

*THINK ABOUT*...a lesson, unit, topic, chapter, or theme. Note some ways to *model, show,* or *demonstrate* to shepherd transfer of the targeted somethings. Include ways to model prior to the lesson (Here's a finished sample), during the lesson to provide needed scaffolding (Notice how this is done), and for short-term and long-term use following the teaching (How does yours compare?).

Focus: *Research*      *Using Note Cards*

### Beginning of the Lesson

*Present an example of the product or process.*

*"I have a prototype for you to use as a generic model. It contains the key elements. Here is how I use a note card."*

### Middle of the Lesson

*Do you have the key elements of the model?*

*"Notice the model note card lists the subject and author for easy cross referencing. How are we using them?"*

### End of the Lesson

*How did you vary from the model? Why?*

*"Notice the variations on the original model. Here are ten different ones. Each one fits the prototype but is unique."*

**NEAR TRANSFER**

### ◆ SOMEHOWS ◆

**HUGGING**

# Modeling
Your Example

***THINK BACK***...to a lesson, unit, topic, chapter, or theme. Note some ways to *model, show,* or *demonstrate* to shepherd transfer of the targeted somethings. Include ways to model prior to the lesson (Here's a finished sample), during the lesson to provide needed scaffolding (Notice how this is done), and for short-term and long-term use following the teaching (How does yours compare?). ***Redesign*** with modeling to hug for the desired transfer.

*Focus:*

### Beginning of the Lesson

*Present an example of the product or process.*

### Middle of the Lesson

*Do you have the key elements of the model?*

### End of the Lesson

*How did you vary from the model? Why?*

**NEAR TRANSFER**

**The Somehows of Transfer**

◆ S O M E H O W S ◆

**HUGGING**

# Modeling
### Your Example

*THINK AHEAD*...to a lesson, unit, topic, chapter, or theme. Note some ways to *model, show*, or *demonstrate* to shepherd transfer of the targeted somethings. Include ways to model prior to the lesson (Here's a finished sample), during the lesson to provide needed scaffolding (Notice how this is done), and for short-term and long-term use following the teaching (How does yours compare?). *Design* with modeling to hug for the desired transfer.

*Focus:*

### Beginning of the Lesson

*Present an example of the product or process.*

### Middle of the Lesson

*Do you have the key elements of the model?*

### End of the Lesson

*How did you vary from the model? Why?*

NEAR TRANSFER

### ◆ SOMEHOWS ◆

**HUGGING**

# Modeling
## Your Example

***THINK AGAIN...***of a lesson, unit, topic, chapter, or theme. Note some ways to ***model, show,*** or ***demonstrate*** to shepherd transfer of the targeted somethings. Include ways to model prior to the lesson (Here's a finished sample), during the lesson to provide needed scaffolding (Notice how this is done), and for short-term and long-term use following the teaching (How does yours compare?). ***Refine*** with modeling to hug for the desired transfer.

*Focus:*

**Beginning of the Lesson**

*Present an example of the product or process.*

**Middle of the Lesson**

*Do you have the key elements of the model?*

**End of the Lesson**

*How did you vary from the model? Why?*

**NEAR TRANSFER**

The Somehows of Transfer

# ◆ INSPIRATIONS ◆

◆ S O M E H O W S ◆

**HUGGING**

# Problem-based Learning
"Learning content through solving problems"

Method 5

**DEFINITION**—engaging students in learning a body of facts, concepts, ideas, and/or procedures through active, open-ended problem solving; placing students first in problematic situations; immersing them in the experience in order to pull together relevant information; developing *active* rather than *inert* knowledge.

Problem-based learning is a hugging strategy because its philosophy is, "If you want active use of knowledge later, build active use of knowledge into the learning process."

## LESSON EXAMPLE

Problem-based learning can be done inductively or deductively. In the inductive approach, problems are presented at the outset and students use sources to assemble the knowledge necessary. For example, chemistry students might be given a mystery chemical along with a source book about various tests to perform and challenged to figure out what the substance is. In the deductive approach, some knowledge is provided at the outset, with the students then engaging in open-ended problem solving that requires using the knowledge. For example, students might learn about the literary form of haiku and then compose their own.

## VERBAL CUES

- "Here's the situation . . ."
- "What do you know?"
- "What can you do?"
- "What is the goal?"
- "How can you accomplish the task?"

## METHODS

- Identify problematic situation
- Engage in problem solving

**NEAR TRANSFER**

◆ S O M E H O W S ◆

**HUGGING**

# Problem-based Learning
### A Sample

***THINK ABOUT***...a lesson, unit, topic, chapter, or theme. Note the opportunities to *create problematic situations or construct experiential episodes or field work in which students pull together or locate relevant information* to shepherd transfer of the targeted somethings. Include: prototypical scenarios (set up a mock trial or voyage); real-life experiences (outdoor education); and field work (taking over as principal for the day).

Focus: *Social Studies   Discrimination and Reconstruction*

### Beginning of the Lesson

How can I create a problem-solving situation?

*Introduce students to the reconstruction period and divide them into groups representing various constituencies, for instance carpetbaggers, poor blacks, etc. Set up a conflict between, for example, a rich landowner and his farm laborers.*

### Middle of the Lesson

Monitor the experience for universal learnings.

*The students meet in their groups to promote their special interests. They must develop a plan for collective action, drawing on information about the historical circumstances from their text and other sources.*

### End of the Lesson

How does this help us understand?

*Representatives from different groups engage in interactions around issues such as land ownership, where they defend their interests.*

**NEAR TRANSFER**

HOW TO TEACH FOR TRANSFER

◆ S O M E H O W S ◆

**HUGGING**

# Problem-based Learning
Your Example

*THINK BACK...to a lesson, unit, topic, chapter, or theme. Note the opportunities to **create problematic situations or construct experiential episodes or field work in which students pull together or locate relevant information** to shepherd transfer of the targeted somethings. Include: prototypical scenarios (set up a mock trial or voyage); real-life experiences (outdoor education); and field work (taking over as principal for the day). **Redesign** for transfer of the targeted somethings.*

*Focus:*

### Beginning of the Lesson

*How can I create a problem-solving situation?*

### Middle of the Lesson

*Monitor the experience for universal learnings.*

### End of the Lesson

*How does this help us understand?*

**NEAR TRANSFER**

The Somehows of Transfer

◆ S O M E H O W S ◆

### HUGGING

# Problem-based Learning
## Your Example

*THINK AHEAD*...to a lesson, unit, topic, chapter, or theme. Note the opportunities to *create problematic situations or construct experiential episodes or field work in which students pull together or locate relevant information* to shepherd transfer of the targeted somethings. Include: prototypical scenarios (set up a mock trial or voyage); real-life experiences (outdoor education); and field work (taking over as principal for the day). *Design* for transfer of the targeted somethings.

*Focus:*

### Beginning of the Lesson

*How can I create a problem-solving situation?*

### Middle of the Lesson

*Monitor the experience for universal learnings.*

### End of the Lesson

*How does this help us understand?*

NEAR TRANSFER

## ◆ SOMEHOWS ◆

### HUGGING

# Problem-based Learning
### Your Example

***THINK AGAIN***...of a lesson, unit, topic, chapter, or theme. Note the opportunities to *create problematic situations or construct experiential episodes or field work in which students pull together or locate relevant information* to shepherd transfer of the targeted somethings. Include: prototypical scenarios (set up a mock trial or voyage); real-life experiences (outdoor education); and field work (taking over as principal for the day). ***Refine*** for transfer of the targeted somethings.

*Focus:*

### Beginning of the Lesson

*How can I create a problem-solving situation?*

### Middle of the Lesson

*Monitor the experience for universal learnings.*

### End of the Lesson

*How does this help us understand?*

### NEAR TRANSFER

♦ INSPIRATIONS ♦

# MEDIATING TRANSFER: BRIDGING STRATEGIES

- *Anticipating Applications*: Scouting for relevant uses

- *Generalizing Concepts*: Extrapolating generic ideas

- *Using Analogies*: Comparing; finding similarities

- *Parallel Problem Solving*: Similar problems in different contexts

- *Metacognitive Reflection*: Thinking about thinking; planning, monitoring, evaluating

## Far Transfer/High Road/Bridging

**FAR TRANSFER**   A rough distinction is drawn between "near transfer" and "far transfer." Far transfer refers to transfer between contexts that are very different. Here are some examples of far transfer:

- Using problem-solving skills acquired in mathematics to puzzle out an exercise in English.
- Using knowledge of history to better understand current events unfolding in the daily paper.
- Using knowledge from literature to think about your own life situations.

**HIGH ROAD TRANSFER**   High road transfer is one of two fundamental mechanisms of transfer identified by Gavriel Salomon and David Perkins. High road transfer occurs through mindful abstraction or decontextualization of knowledge or skills for application in another context. It is a thoughtful, effort-demanding process, intellectual in character.

High road transfer is particularly important as a way of achieving far transfer because it readily bridges large gaps.

- A student abstracts from mathematics studies some diagramming strategies for representing problems; the student applies these diagramming strategies in English to understand the structure of a story.
- In English class, a student notices how two siblings in a novel treat one another, sometimes getting along, sometimes not getting along; the student becomes more mindful about interactions at home with a sibling, improving the relationship.

◆ SOMEHOWS ◆

- A student learns about the principle of entropy in physics. The student abstracts the general idea that random events tend to lead to an accumulation of haphazardness, and recognizes that entropy is at work in making his or her desk and class notes messy.

**BRIDGING** This is a general term for teaching techniques that foster transfer by engaging learners in mindfully abstracting knowledge and skills from one context and applying them in another. Bridging asks the learner to think about what is being learned, generalize it, and anticipate applications. Alternatively, bridging asks the learner to think about the current situation, generalize its needs, and "bridge backwards" to recall already-learned knowledge and skills that might apply.

Bridging relies on the mechanism of "high road transfer." Teachers can help learners to bridge by conducting discussions and setting up activities that encourage them to do so. Also, students can learn to be "self-bridgers," autonomously abstracting and transferring as a learning skill.

Several specific instructional techniques for bridging are listed at the opening of this section on high road transfer strategies that bridge for far transfer.

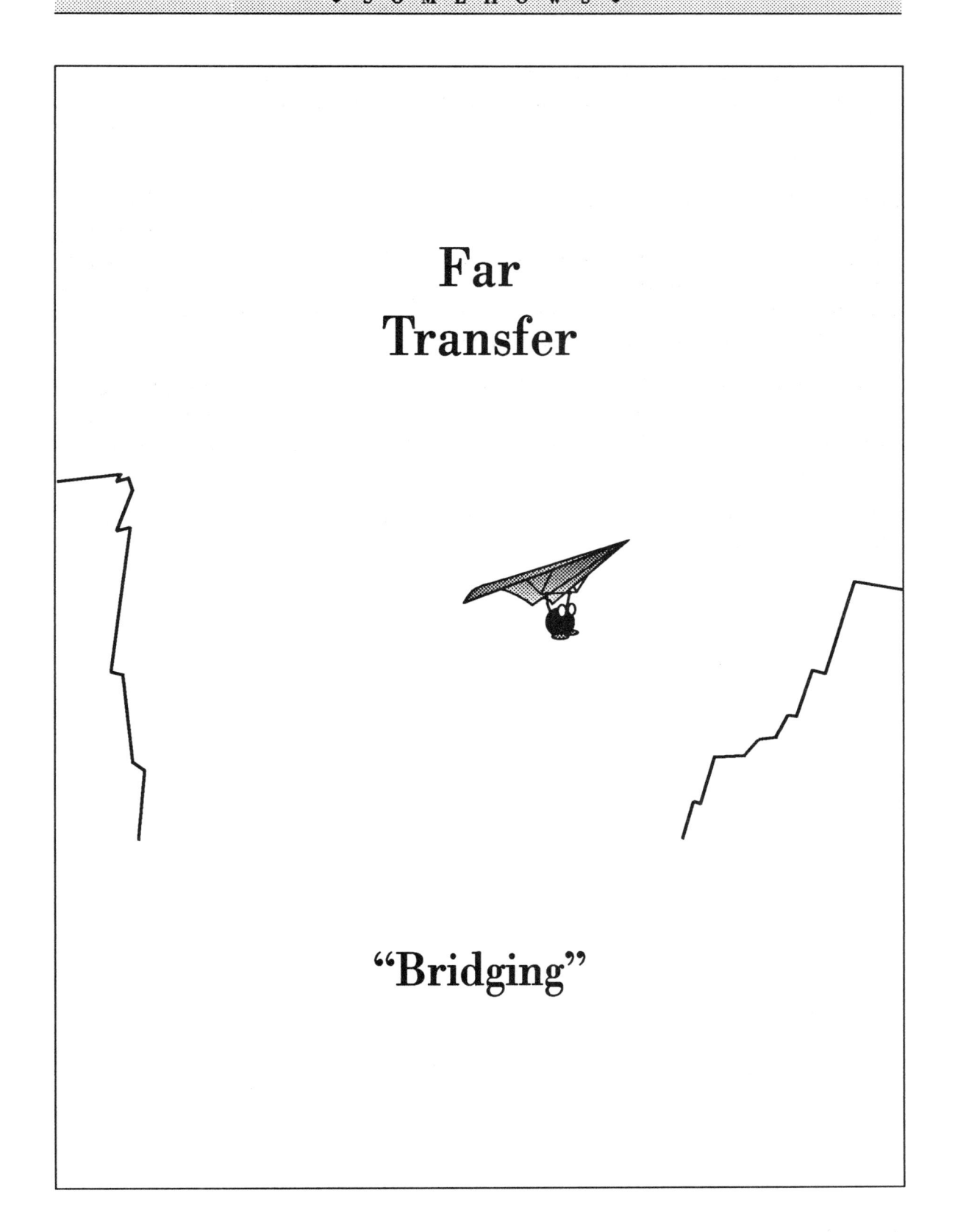

## ◆ SOMEHOWS ◆

# Far Transfer

## "Bridging"

### ◆ INSPIRATIONS ◆

**SOMEHOWS**

**BRIDGING**

> Method
> **6**

# Anticipating Applications
### "Scouting For Relevant Uses"

**DEFINITION**—thinking about an upcoming opportunity to use the new idea in a different context; thinking about an adjustment that will make an application more relevant; targeting future diverse applications rather than expecting spontaneous transfer.

### LESSON EXAMPLE
After working on the division of fractions, guide students to project possible future uses of the skill in different contexts. Ask students, "How might you use this idea in other subject areas or in life outside school?"

### VERBAL CUES
- "How might you use this?"
- "What if you adapted it this way?"
- "Do you see any opportunities to try this out?"
- "Can you think of an application?"
- "Have you seen this used somewhere else?"

### METHODS
Cue application thinking by asking how the ideas can be used:
- in another class;
- in life situations; or
- in past circumstances.

**FAR TRANSFER**

The Somehows of Transfer

◆ S O M E H O W S ◆

**BRIDGING**

# Anticipating Applications
## A Sample

**THINK ABOUT**...a lesson, unit, topic, chapter, or theme. Note opportunities to *anticipate applications; predict future use; scout for relevant transfer; or speculate on applications* to shepherd transfer of the targeted somethings. Include: ways to anticipate applications (How might you use this in science class?); ways to predict future use (Imagine using this when ____.); ways to scout for relevant transfer (Brainstorm or survey others for possible uses of this ___. Where might it apply?).

Focus: *Science*          *Solar System*

### Beginning of the Lesson

How might we use this elsewhere?

*Have student groups (3-5) think about and record how they might use "somethings" about the solar system in other classes (e.g., one group focuses on math class by comparing size, distance, etc.*

### Middle of the Lesson

Look for ways to use this beyond this science class.

*As students become involved in the study, use them as conduits for transfer — have them interview teachers in various subjects to gather ideas about relevant transfer and use.*

### End of the Lesson

Where can we apply this in life?

*Foster reflective thinking in journals by having students write down one projected use of "somethings" they learned about the solar system.*

**FAR TRANSFER**

68   HOW TO TEACH FOR TRANSFER

◆ S O M E H O W S ◆

**BRIDGING**

# Anticipating Applications
## Your Example

*THINK BACK*...to a lesson, unit, topic, chapter, or theme. Note opportunities to ***anticipate applications; predict future use; scout for relevant transfer; or speculate on applications*** to shepherd transfer of the targeted somethings. Include: ways to anticipate applications (How might you use this in science class?); ways to predict future use (Imagine using this when ____.); ways to scout for relevant transfer (Brainstorm or survey others for possible uses of this ___. Where might it apply?). ***Redesign*** applications to bridge for transfer.

*Focus:*

### Beginning of the Lesson
*How might we use this elsewhere?*

### Middle of the Lesson
*Look for ways to use this beyond this science class.*

### End of the Lesson
*Where can we apply this in life?*

**FAR TRANSFER**

◆ SOMEHOWS ◆

**BRIDGING**

# Anticipating Applications
## Your Example

***THINK AHEAD***...to a lesson, unit, topic, chapter, or theme. Note opportunities to *anticipate applications; predict future use; scout for relevant transfer; or speculate on applications* to shepherd transfer of the targeted somethings. Include: ways to anticipate applications (How might you use this in science class?); ways to predict future use (Imagine using this when ____.); ways to scout for relevant transfer (Brainstorm or survey others for possible uses of this ___. Where might it apply?). *Design* applications to bridge for transfer.

*Focus:*

### Beginning of the Lesson

*How might we use this elsewhere?*

### Middle of the Lesson

*Look for ways to use this beyond this science class.*

### End of the Lesson

*Where can we apply this in life?*

**FAR TRANSFER**

◆ SOMEHOWS ◆

## BRIDGING

# Anticipating Applications
Your Example

*THINK AGAIN*...of a lesson, unit, topic, chapter, or theme. Note opportunities to *anticipate applications; predict future use; scout for relevant transfer; or speculate on applications* to shepherd transfer of the targeted somethings. Include: ways to anticipate applications (How might you use this in science class?); ways to predict future use (Imagine using this when ____.); ways to scout for relevant transfer (Brainstorm or survey others for possible uses of this ___. Where might it apply?). *Refine* applications to bridge for transfer.

*Focus:*

### Beginning of the Lesson

*How might we use this elsewhere?*

### Middle of the Lesson

*Look for ways to use this beyond this science class.*

### End of the Lesson

*Where can we apply this in life?*

FAR TRANSFER

The Somehows of Transfer

♦ INSPIRATIONS ♦

◆ S O M E H O W S ◆

**BRIDGING**

# Method 7

## Generalizing Concepts
"Extrapolating Generic Ideas"

**DEFINITION**—asking students to pull the generic piece out of a situation; encouraging them to generalize concepts by applying them universally; looking for principles, underlying truths, or "big ideas."

### LESSON EXAMPLE

As students learn geometry, ask them to reflect on their own problem-solving processes and to generalize about elements of those processes that seem to help. For instance, students might say, "Use a diagram." Then ask, "Is that generally useful in other situations? How? Why? Give me some specific examples."

### VERBAL CUES
- "What big ideas can you pull from this?"
- "What truths seem apparent?"
- "What's the real lesson?"
- "Is there a rule, law, or principle here?"
- "Can we say that 'Generally speaking . . .' ?"

### METHODS
- Identify key attributes.
- Look for the "big ideas."
- Try to sift out the generic ideas.
- Use concept maps — (concepts in center are "big ideas").

**FAR TRANSFER**

The Somehows of Transfer

◆ S O M E H O W S ◆

## BRIDGING

# Generalizing Concepts
### A Sample

*THINK ABOUT...a lesson, unit, topic, chapter, or theme. Note opportunities to **generalize concepts; pull out the generic piece; apply universally; find underlying truths or "big ideas"** to shepherd transfer of the targeted somethings. Include ways to pull out the generic piece (What is a common thread running through both stories?); ways to apply universally (What is the moral or lesson here?); ways to find underlying truths (Find a meaningful quote for this); ways to highlight the "big ideas" (What is the most important thing to remember here?).*

*Focus:* Outdoor Education     Cemetery Study

### Beginning of the Lesson

*Be alert to key characteristics.*

Ask students to do a KWL (see glossary) of what they know about cemeteries. Then ask them to pull out several generalizations (e.g., the families all together).

### Middle of the Lesson

*What ideas seem to have transfer potential?*

As students are working in the cemetery, have them use a guide sheet to gather data — suggest a "memoing technique" in which they jot down (or make a memo of) generalizations that occur (e.g., ethnic groups have separate sections in the cemetery).

### End of the Lesson

*What are the big ideas that we can use?*

Ask students to work with partners and develop a list of generalizations on "big ideas" from their cemetery study.

## FAR TRANSFER

◆ SOMEHOWS ◆

**BRIDGING**

# Generalizing Concepts
Your Example

*THINK ABOUT*...a lesson, unit, topic, chapter, or theme. Note opportunities to *generalize concepts; pull out the generic piece; apply universally; find underlying truths or "big ideas"* to shepherd transfer of the targeted somethings. Include ways to pull out the generic piece (What is a common thread running through both stories?); ways to apply universally (What is the moral or lesson here?); ways to find underlying truths (Find a meaningful quote for this); ways to highlight the "big ideas" (What is the most important thing to remember here?). *Redesign* for transfer.

*Focus:*

### Beginning of the Lesson

*Be alert to key characteristics.*

### Middle of the Lesson

*What ideas seem to have transfer potential?*

### End of the Lesson

*What are the big ideas that we can use?*

**FAR TRANSFER**

The Somehows of Transfer

◆ S O M E H O W S ◆

**BRIDGING**

# Generalizing Concepts
Your Example

*THINK AHEAD...to a lesson, unit, topic, chapter, or theme. Note opportunities to **generalize concepts; pull out the generic piece; apply universally; find underlying truths or "big ideas"** to shepherd transfer of the targeted somethings. Include ways to pull out the generic piece (What is a common thread running through both stories?); ways to apply universally (What is the moral or lesson here?); ways to find underlying truths (Find a meaningful quote for this); ways to highlight the "big ideas" (What is the most important thing to remember here?). **Design** for transfer.*
*Focus:*

### Beginning of the Lesson
*Be alert to key characteristics.*

### Middle of the Lesson
*What ideas seem to have transfer potential?*

### End of the Lesson
*What are the big ideas that we can use?*

**FAR TRANSFER**

HOW TO TEACH FOR TRANSFER

◆ S O M E H O W S ◆

**BRIDGING**

# Generalizing Concepts
## Your Example

***THINK AGAIN***...of a lesson, unit, topic, chapter, or theme. Note opportunities to *generalize concepts; pull out the generic piece; apply universally; find underlying truths or "big ideas"* to shepherd transfer of the targeted somethings. Include ways to pull out the generic piece (What is a common thread running through both stories?); ways to apply universally (What is the moral or lesson here?); ways to find underlying truths (Find a meaningful quote for this); ways to highlight the "big ideas" (What is the most important thing to remember here?). *Refine* for transfer.

*Focus:*

### Beginning of the Lesson

*Be alert to key characteristics.*

### Middle of the Lesson

*What ideas seem to have transfer potential?*

### End of the Lesson

*What are the big ideas that we can use?*

**FAR TRANSFER**

♦ INSPIRATIONS ♦

**◆ S O M E H O W S ◆**

**BRIDGING**

**Method 8**

# Using Analogies
"Comparing, Finding Similarities"

**DEFINITION**—finding or creating and analyzing analogies; comparing; using metaphors; making creative connections.

### LESSON EXAMPLE

Have students compare courage and rain. ("For example, courage is like the rain. Both can come on you unexpectedly.") Have students discuss how the "unexpectedness" of a courageous act is similar to the "unexpectedness" of a summer shower. Analyze this analogy and engage students in a discussion about courage that unpacks the analogy by elaborating and extending the thinking and explicitly forcing transfer through systematic comparison.

### VERBAL CUES

- "How is ____ like ____?"
- "____ is like ____ because both ____."
- "____ : ____ :: ____ : ____"
- "Compare _____ to _____."
- "Find the similarities in _____ as compared to _____."
                        (abstract)                    (concrete)

### METHODS

- Create analogies, metaphors, and similes.
- Analyze analogies, metaphors, and similes.

**FAR TRANSFER**

**The Somehows of Transfer**

♦ S O M E H O W S ♦

**BRIDGING**

# Using Analogies
## A Sample

*THINK ABOUT...* a lesson, unit, topic, chapter, or theme. Note opportunities to *use analogies; analyze analogies; compare and create metaphors; and make creative connections* to shepherd transfer of the targeted somethings. Include ways to use analogies (How is an atom like the solar system?); ways to analyze analogies (Let's examine all the ways a suitcase is like fear. The handle is like the grip it has on you.); ways to compare metaphors (Describe how a good book is like a summer romance.); ways to make creative connections (Both thinking and golf require a clear direction.).

Focus: *Language Arts*   *Poetry: Span of Life*

### Beginning of the Lesson

*Think how the topic is like something else.*

*Ask students to complete:*
*Dogs are like people because both ____.*

### Middle of the Lesson

*What similarities are you noticing?*

*"The old dog barks backwards without standing up. I remember when he was a pup." — Robert Frost*
*Ask students to compare what Frost says about the dog's shifts in behavior over its life span with their own behavior.*

### End of the Lesson

*Analyze these metaphors.*

*Ask students to analyze one of these metaphors — the autumn of his life, the twilight years, the sunset of his days.*

**FAR TRANSFER**

## ◆ SOMEHOWS ◆

### BRIDGING

# Using Analogies
### Your Example

***THINK BACK***...to a lesson, unit, topic, chapter, or theme. Note opportunities to *use analogies; analyze analogies; compare and create metaphors; and make creative connections* to shepherd transfer of the targeted somethings. Include ways to use analogies (How is an atom like the solar system?); ways to analyze analogies (Let's examine all the ways a suitcase is like fear. The handle is like the grip it has on you.); ways to compare metaphors (Describe how a good book is like a summer romance.); ways to make creative connections (Both thinking and golf require a clear direction.). ***Redesign*** for transfer.

*Focus:*

### Beginning of the Lesson

*Think how the topic is like something else.*

### Middle of the Lesson

*What similarities are you noticing?*

### End of the Lesson

*Analyze these metaphors.*

### FAR TRANSFER

◆ S O M E H O W S ◆

**BRIDGING**

# Using Analogies
## Your Example

*THINK AHEAD*...to a lesson, unit, topic, chapter, or theme. Note opportunities to *use analogies; analyze analogies; compare and create metaphors; and make creative connections* to shepherd transfer of the targeted somethings. Include ways to use analogies (How is an atom like the solar system?); ways to analyze analogies (Let's examine all the ways a suitcase is like fear. The handle is like the grip it has on you.); ways to compare metaphors (Describe how a good book is like a summer romance.); ways to make connections (Both thinking and golf require a clear direction.). *Design* for transfer.
*Focus:*

### Beginning of the Lesson

*Think how the topic is like something else.*

### Middle of the Lesson

*What similarities are you noticing?*

### End of the Lesson

*Analyze these metaphors.*

**FAR TRANSFER**

**◆ SOMEHOWS ◆**

**BRIDGING**

# Using Analogies
## Your Example

*THINK AGAIN...*of a lesson, unit, topic, chapter, or theme. Note opportunities to *use analogies; analyze analogies; compare and create metaphors; and make creative connections* to shepherd transfer of the targeted somethings. Include ways to use analogies (How is an atom like the solar system?); ways to analyze analogies (Let's examine all the ways a suitcase is like fear. The handle is like the grip it has on you.); ways to compare metaphors (Describe how a good book is like a summer romance.); ways to make creative connections (Both thinking and golf require a clear direction.). *Refine* for transfer.

*Focus:*

### Beginning of the Lesson

*Think how the topic is like something else.*

### Middle of the Lesson

*What similarities are you noticing?*

### End of the Lesson

*Analyze these metaphors.*

**FAR TRANSFER**

The Somehows of Transfer

♦ I N S P I R A T I O N S ♦

## ◆ SOMEHOWS ◆

### BRIDGING

# Parallel Problem Solving
### "Similar problems in different contexts"

**Method 9**

**DEFINITION**—solving problems with parallel structure and content in two different areas; gaining an appreciation for the similarities and contrasts between areas. (Often, although not necessarily, one of the areas concerns personal or everyday life.)

### LESSON EXAMPLE
Have students take a global or historic problem into the context of their personal lives to help them understand the more abstract global problem. For example, during the American Revolution the colonists did not want to be taxed. They were in conflict with the mother country. Ask students, "What do you do when you're in conflict with your mother? She wants you to eat your peas and you hate peas. What do you do? Boycott? Retreat? Throw a temper tantrum? What strategies do you use? How do these compare to the strategies the colonists used?

### VERBAL CUES
- "Do you see the parallels to your own situation?"
- "How is this like personal life?"
- "Can you relate to this personally?"
- "Does this sound familiar?"
- "Do you see any similarities to your own life to problems in other subjects?"

### METHODS
Establish a problematic situation that parallels essential conflict within subject matter.

### FAR TRANSFER

The Somehows of Transfer

◆ S O M E H O W S ◆

**BRIDGING**

# Parallel Problem Solving
## A Sample

**THINK ABOUT**...a lesson, unit, topic, chapter, or theme. Note ways to *structure parallel problems; associate one idea with a similar idea; parallel a personal situation with a similar, but more universal situation* to shepherd transfer of the targeted somethings. Include: ways to structure parallel problems (Think of a personal instance when you were afraid to ask. What did you do?); ways to associate one idea with a similar idea (What does this remind you of?); ways to parallel personal situations with similar but more universal situations (Compare the structure of our presidency to the English monarchy.).

Focus: *Language Arts*   *Lord of the Flies: Social Order*

### Beginning of the Lesson

Think of a similar conflict situation.

*Elicit examples from personal situations in which students experienced lack of any social order (e.g., substitute teacher in Jr. High class).*

### Middle of the Lesson

How are these situations similar/dissimilar?

*Ask students to associate the chaos in Lord of the Flies with a personal experience and a global incident and tell how all three are similar.*

### End of the Lesson

How do our learnings in one situation transfer to the other?

*Have students problem-solve incidents in the novel based on their own experiences and tell how they might detour from the characters' actions.*

**FAR TRANSFER**

## ◆ SOMEHOWS ◆

### BRIDGING

# Parallel Problem Solving
## Your Example

*THINK BACK...* to a lesson, unit, topic, chapter, or theme. Note ways to *structure parallel problems; associate one idea with a similar idea; parallel a personal situation with a similar, but more universal situation* to shepherd transfer of the targeted somethings. Include: ways to structure parallel problems (Think of a personal instance when you were afraid to ask. What did you do?); ways to associate one idea with a similar idea (What does this remind you of?); ways to parallel personal situations with similar but more universal situations (Compare the structure of our presidency to the English monarchy.). *Redesign* for transfer to the targeted somethings.

*Focus:*

### Beginning of the Lesson

*Think of a similar conflict situation.*

### Middle of the Lesson

*How are these situations similar/dissimilar?*

### End of the Lesson

*How do our learnings in one situation transfer to the other?*

### FAR TRANSFER

## BRIDGING

# Parallel Problem Solving
### Your Example

*THINK AHEAD*...to a lesson, unit, topic, chapter, or theme. Note ways to *structure parallel problems; associate one idea with a similar idea; parallel a personal situation with a similar, but more universal situation* to shepherd transfer of the targeted somethings. Include: ways to structure parallel problems (Think of a personal instance when you were afraid to ask. What did you do?); ways to associate one idea with a similar idea (What does this remind you of?); ways to parallel personal situations with similar but more universal situations (Compare the structure of our presidency to the English monarchy.). *Design* for transfer to the targeted somethings.

*Focus:*

### Beginning of the Lesson

*Think of a similar conflict situation.*

### Middle of the Lesson

*How are these situations similar/dissimilar?*

### End of the Lesson

*How do our learnings in one situation transfer to the other?*

FAR TRANSFER

### ◆ SOMEHOWS ◆

## BRIDGING

# Parallel Problem Solving
## Your Example

*THINK AGAIN...* of a lesson, unit, topic, chapter, or theme. Note ways to *structure parallel problems; associate one idea with a similar idea; parallel a personal situation with a similar, but more universal situation* to shepherd transfer of the targeted somethings. Include: ways to structure parallel problems (Think of a personal instance when you were afraid to ask. What did you do?); ways to associate one idea with a similar idea (What does this remind you of?); ways to parallel personal situations with similar but more universal situations (Compare the structure of our presidency to the English monarchy.). *Refine* for transfer to the targeted somethings.

*Focus:*

### Beginning of the Lesson

*Think of a similar conflict situation.*

### Middle of the Lesson

*How are these situations similar/dissimilar?*

### End of the Lesson

*How do our learnings in one situation transfer to the other?*

**FAR TRANSFER**

The Somehows of Transfer

♦ INSPIRATIONS ♦

◆ SOMEHOWS ◆

**BRIDGING**

# Method 10

## Metacognitive Reflection
"Thinking about Thinking; Planning, Monitoring, Evaluating"

**DEFINITION**—planning, monitoring, and evaluating one's own thinking; being aware and controlling one's own thinking and behavior; thinking about thinking; aware, strategic, and reflective use of thinking about thinking; thinking about how to approach a task this time or how to do better next time.

### LESSON EXAMPLE
After completing a series of math problems on the associative principle, ask students to think about how they attacked the problems. Ask, "What was the problem here? What things were similar across problems? What were your strategies? What did you do first? Form images? Relate to other problems? What were the stumpers?" Have students evaluate their own performance as they think about their thinking strategies and become aware of their own behavior.

### VERBAL CUES
- "What is your goal?"
- "Track your steps in this."
- "Monitor your progress."
- "Look back and evaluate your work."
- "What would you do the same or differently next time?"

### METHODS
- Journals
- Paired partners thinking aloud
- Generate own rules
- Plus, Minus, Interesting (PMI) charts

**FAR TRANSFER**

◆ S O M E H O W S ◆

### BRIDGING

# Metacognitive Reflection
## A Sample

THINK ABOUT...a lesson, unit, topic, chapter, or theme. Note opportunities to *reflect on one's own behavior; plan ahead; monitor or track one's progress; or map or evaluate one's thinking and behavior* to shepherd transfer to targeted somethings. Include: ways to plan ahead (How will you approach this topic?); ways to monitor or track (Periodically check your progress by comparing notes with your partner.); ways to strategically map one's procedure (Mark your stumbling blocks on a chart.); reflective evaluation (Look back and comment on your strengths and weaknesses in this effort.).

Focus: *Math*   *Mental Movies: The Pizza Problem*

### Beginning of the Lesson

How can I engage students in planning an approach?

*Present this problem and ask small groups of students to make a "mental movie" depicting the information. [Jack buys two pizzas. He eats 1/3 of what he got. Jim eats 2/5 of the remainder. Then Jack eats 1/2 of what's left. How much is left over for Jane to eat?]*

### Middle of the Lesson

How will students monitor their progress?

*Have several groups exchange "blow-by-blow" accounts and revise and refine theirs.*

### End of the Lesson

How will students reflect and evaluate their progress?

*Ask them to reflect on the pluses and minuses of the "mental movies" strategy.*

### FAR TRANSFER

◆ S O M E H O W S ◆

**BRIDGING**

# Metacognitive Reflection
## Your Example

*THINK BACK...* to a lesson, unit, topic, chapter, or theme. Note opportunities to *reflect on one's own behavior; plan ahead; monitor or track one's progress; or map or evaluate one's thinking and behavior* to shepherd transfer to targeted somethings. Include: ways to plan ahead (How will you approach this topic?); ways to monitor or track (Periodically check your progress by comparing notes with your partner.); ways to strategically map one's procedure (Mark your stumbling blocks on a chart.); reflective evaluation (Look back and comment on your strengths and weaknesses in this effort.). *Redesign* for transfer to the targeted somethings.

*Focus:*

### Beginning of the Lesson

*How can I engage students in planning an approach?*

### Middle of the Lesson

*How will students monitor their progress?*

### End of the Lesson

*How will students reflect and evaluate their progress?*

**FAR TRANSFER**

◆ S O M E H O W S ◆

**BRIDGING**

# Metacognitive Reflection
## Your Example

*THINK AHEAD*...to a lesson, unit, topic, chapter, or theme. Note opportunities to ***reflect on one's own behavior; plan ahead; monitor or track one's progress; or map or evaluate one's thinking and behavior*** to shepherd transfer to targeted somethings. Include: ways to plan ahead (How will you approach this topic?); ways to monitor or track (Periodically check your progress by comparing notes with your partner.); ways to strategically map one's procedure (Mark your stumbling blocks on a chart.); reflective evaluation (Look back and comment on your strengths and weaknesses in this effort.). ***Design*** for transfer to the targeted somethings.

*Focus:*

### Beginning of the Lesson

*How can I engage students in planning an approach?*

### Middle of the Lesson

*How will students monitor their progress?*

### End of the Lesson

*How will students reflect and evaluate their progress?*

**FAR TRANSFER**

HOW TO TEACH FOR TRANSFER

◆ S O M E H O W S ◆

**BRIDGING**

# Metacognitive Reflection
Your Example

*THINK AGAIN...of a lesson, unit, topic, chapter, or theme. Note opportunities to **reflect on one's own behavior; plan ahead; monitor or track one's progress; or map or evaluate one's thinking and behavior** to shepherd transfer to targeted somethings. Include: ways to plan ahead (How will you approach this topic?); ways to monitor or track (Periodically check your progress by comparing notes with your partner.); ways to strategically map one's procedure (Mark your stumbling blocks on a chart.); reflective evaluation (Look back and comment on your strengths and weaknesses in this effort.). **Refine** for transfer to the targeted somethings.*
*Focus:*

### Beginning of the Lesson
*How can I engage students in planning an approach?*

### Middle of the Lesson
*How will students monitor their progress?*

### End of the Lesson
*How will students reflect and evaluate their progress?*

**FAR TRANSFER**

The Somehows of Transfer

# The "Somewheres" of Transfer

*Our mission as educators is to help every child become a more active, engaged, committed, and skillful learner, not just for a test, but for a lifetime.*

—James Bellanca

## TARGETING THE "SOMEWHERES" OF TRANSFER

By asking students to think back to an experience or think ahead to a possible application, the teacher targets the *somewheres* for future transfer.

LITERATURE TEACHER: In *The Old Man and the Sea*, Hemingway presents an impressive characterization of a man who perseveres against tremendous odds. Take a moment to think back to a time in your life when you used your will power to stick to something and see it through.

(After a minute or two of silence) Now, share your stories with a partner.

DENNIS: (turning to Louisa) Once when I was really little I climbed a tree and when I was trying to get down I slipped and ended up clutching onto this branch. I had to hold on really tight for a long time while my brother went to get the ladder. It seemed like forever.

LOUISA: I remember once when I forced myself to finish my social studies project because it was due the next day. I had to paint this salt and flour relief map. It was a lot of fun when I started—but boy did I get sick of it! I think that was hard to do—just like the old man's struggle with the marlin.

# CHAPTER 3

LITERATURE TEACHER: Now, go to your logs and think ahead. Write a sentence or two about how this ability to persevere will help you in another class. For example, when will persevering help you in math class or in the science lab? Be specific. Target an upcoming assignment for another subject area that is going to take lots of will power and "stick-to-it-iveness" to get it done. Try to think about how you can use this persevering attitude in other places. See if you can transfer it across to another subject.

JOSE: (writing in his log) The algebra problems are really hard for me right now. If I don't give up so easily—if I stick with them longer, like the old man—maybe I can get through them.

## THE "SOMEWHERES" OF TRANSFER: WITHIN / ACROSS / INTO

The *somewheres* of transfer are the targets of the *somethings* and the *somehows*. Learning in one situation that is used in another situation is called *transfer*. This transfer may occur within the content being taught, across disciplines to other subject matter, or into life situations. (Conversely, of course, life experiences can transfer into school learning.)

Even to suggest that one would teach something (or learn something) with no expectation for transfer or use is ludicrous. However, research suggests that this transfer of learning, if "left alone" as in the "Bo Peep" theory may not occur as spontaneously or as regularly as we would like. However, when the transfer is shepherded, the likelihood of relevant application and use increases quite dramatically. In order to shepherd or mediate for transfer, we use hugging or bridging strategies that engage students in the desired behavior.

◆ SOMEWHERES ◆

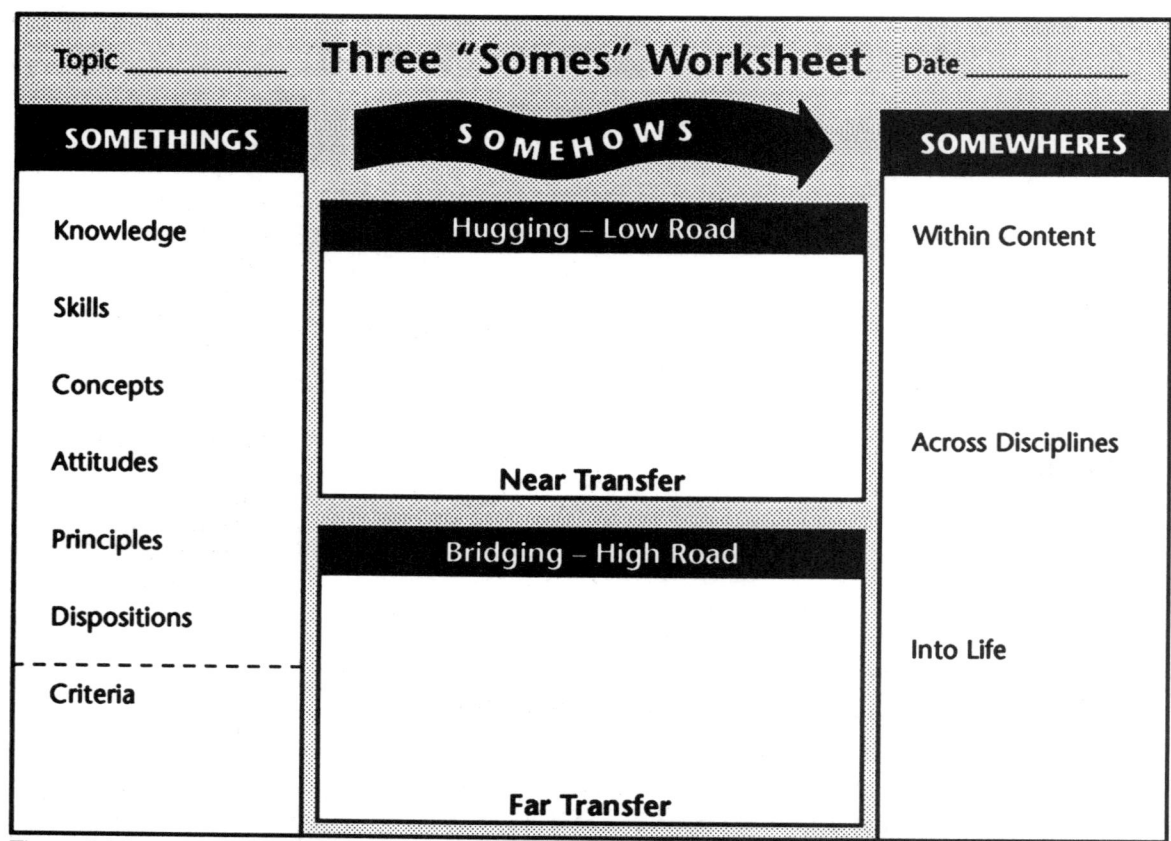

| Topic _____ | Three "Somes" Worksheet | Date _____ |
|---|---|---|
| **SOMETHINGS** | **SOMEHOWS** ➤ | **SOMEWHERES** |
| Knowledge | Hugging – Low Road | Within Content |
| Skills | | |
| Concepts | | |
| Attitudes | Near Transfer | Across Disciplines |
| Principles | Bridging – High Road | |
| Dispositions | | Into Life |
| Criteria | Far Transfer | |

**Figure 6** Three "Somes" Worksheet

However, in addition to hugging and bridging, we can provide further support to the learning process by targeting specific *somewheres* (see Figure 6); also, a full-page version of this worksheet appears at the end of this chapter. This additional targeting of the *somewheres* for transfer, within the same context, across disciplines, or into life situations is fairly easy to do.

An example of targeting a *somewhere* for transfer within a similar context is the science teacher who directs students to relate the concept of the life cycle from the plant unit to the metamorphosis of the butterfly in the insect unit. To target a *somewhere* for transfer across subject areas, the math teacher may suggest that students check their hand calculations on the computer during their technology lab period. Similarly, to target a *somewhere* into personal life situations, the global education teacher may cue students to scout the newspapers, magazines, and broadcasts for current illustrations of aggression as an extension of the study of World War II.

Cuing students to target transfer *somewhere* may occur before, during, or following the lesson. Figure 7 makes more detailed suggestions for the designated *somewheres*. In working with the model, the *somewheres* may be general or more context-specific.

◆ SOMEWHERES ◆

## Three "Somes" Worksheet

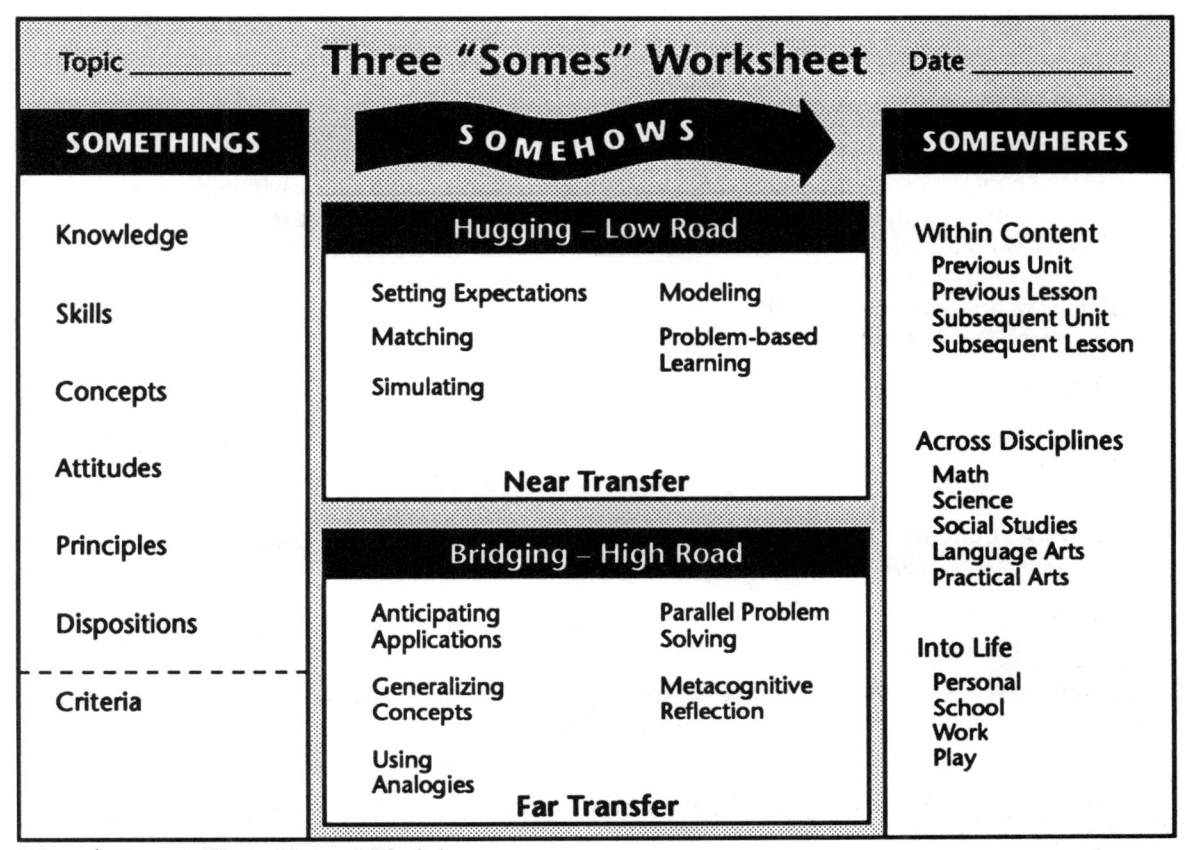

Topic _____    Date _____

| SOMETHINGS | SOMEHOWS | SOMEWHERES |
|---|---|---|
| Knowledge | **Hugging – Low Road** | **Within Content** |
| Skills | Setting Expectations, Modeling | Previous Unit |
| Concepts | Matching, Problem-based Learning | Previous Lesson |
| Attitudes | Simulating | Subsequent Unit |
| Principles | *Near Transfer* | Subsequent Lesson |
| Dispositions | **Bridging – High Road** | **Across Disciplines** |
| — — — — — | Anticipating Applications, Parallel Problem Solving | Math, Science, Social Studies, Language Arts, Practical Arts |
| Criteria | Generalizing Concepts, Metacognitive Reflection | **Into Life** |
|  | Using Analogies | Personal, School, Work, Play |
|  | *Far Transfer* |  |

**Figure 7** Sample Three "Somes" Worksheet

Powerful strategies for promoting the transfer of learning deliberately focus the learner's attention on possible transfer opportunities. Over time, of course, less scaffolding (see glossary) is necessary as the learner takes over the task of finding the *somewheres* for relevant transfer.

# "Somewheres"
## A Sample

*Think About*...a lesson, unit, topic, chapter, or theme. Note opportunities: within the content area, across disciplines, and into life situations to shepherd transfer of the targeted somethings. Include ways to make connections within the same subject matter content (How does this idea connect with what we were talking about yesterday?); ways to use across to another discipline (Think of how you might use this math idea in social studies.); ways to take an idea into a life situation (Cite one way you might use this idea with your friends.).

Focus: *Language Arts  Grammar: Adjectives and Adverbs*
  Within Content: *Continued use in writing own pieces and in reading and inferencing from others' words; becoming precise with language*
  Across Disciplines: *Analyzing for bias in social studies texts, current event news reports; journal articles and editorials*
  Into Life: *Reading menus, brochures, pamphlets, and short commentaries*

Focus:
  Within Content:
  Across Disciplines:
  Into Life:

Focus:
  Within Content:
  Across Disciplines:
  Into Life:

# "Somewheres"
## Your Example

***Think About***...a lesson, unit, topic, chapter, or theme. Note opportunities: within the content area, across disciplines, and into life situations to shepherd transfer of the targeted somethings. Include ways to make connections within the same subject matter content (How does this idea connect with what we were talking about yesterday?); ways to use across to another discipline (Think of how you might use this math idea in social studies.); ways to take an idea into a life situation (Cite one way you might use this idea with your friends.).

### Redesign a lesson by thinking back to "somewheres" just taught

*Focus:*

   Within Content:

   Across Disciplines:

   Into Life:

### Design an upcoming lesson by thinking ahead to "somewheres" to be taught

*Focus:*

   Within Content:

   Across Disciplines:

   Into Life:

### Refine another lesson by thinking again of "somewheres" you plan to teach

*Focus:*

   Within Content:

   Across Disciplines:

   Into Life:

## ASSESSING SITUATIONAL DISPOSITIONS OF TRANSFER

| | | |
|---|---|---|
| SIMPLE / NEAR | OVERLOOKS | Misses appropriate opportunities; overlooks; persists in former ways |
| | DUPLICATES | Performs the drill exactly as practiced; duplicates with no change; copies |
| | REPLICATES | Tailors, but applies in similar situations; replicates |
| | INTEGRATES | Integrates; subtly combines with other ideas and situations; uses with raised consciousness |
| COMPLEX / FAR | MAPS | Carries strategy to other content and into life situations; associates and maps |
| | INNOVATES | Innovates; takes ideas beyond the initial conception; risks; diverges |

**Figure 8 Transfer Continuum**

# ASSESSING TRANSFER

A natural extension of targeting the *somewheres* is, of course, tracking or assessing them. To track the *somewheres*, assess transfer of learning, and evidence that transfer has occurred or is occurring, Fogarty (1990) has developed a model that shows a continuum of transfer behavior. Using this model as a tracking or assessment tool, the teacher can begin to track students' transfer and learners can begin to metacognitively reflect on their own levels of transfer.

The continuum as seen in Figure 8 represents levels of transfer that range from simple or near transfer to more complex or far-reaching transfer. Six distinctions are made: learner dispositions that overlook, duplicate, replicate, integrate, map, or innovate with transfer. Each level comes with a bird metaphor (see Figure 10).

The model needs to be seen in proper perspective. It is not seen as way of assessing a person's general disposition to transfer. How widely a person tries to transfer something learned depends very much on situational variables. For example, student dispositions to internalize and apply ideas, concepts, skills, and attitudes may depend on past knowledge and prior experience (How much background does the student have?); the physical learning environment (Is the climate conducive to learning?); the teaching/learning

> **ASSESSING TRANSFER**
>
> | What We See | What We Hear |
> |---|---|
> | • student work | • student conversations |
> | • collected artifacts | • verbal clues |
> | • concrete evidence | • personal connection making |
> | • graphic representation | • oral articulation |

**Figure 9 Evidence of Transfer**

style match (Is the student enabled by the ways the material is being presented?); the feelings, mood, and emotional state of the student and teacher (Does the student [or teacher] have effective variables that are enhancing or blocking learning?); and innumerable other external and internal influences. In sum, the disposition to transfer may be very situation-dependent, so a person may have a strong disposition to transfer in one situation but not in another. Thus, the continuum is presented simply as a loose framework of "situational dispositions" toward transfer. This model is not intended for judgmental evaluation. Rather, the models are offered as guides to provide insight into student transfer for both the teacher/observer and the student.

As in Figure 9, what we see in student work are, in essence, collected artifacts that provide graphic evidence of transfer. Similarly, what we hear students say gives verbal clues to the personal connection making that goes on. Thus, the teacher seeking evidence of transfer monitors both students' concrete products and their utterances.

In Figure 10, each of the six situational dispositions for transfer is represented both figuratively (metaphor) and graphically (illustration). Each disposition toward transfer is also defined and elaborated with classroom examples of what one might see and hear from students on each level. To know what it looks like and what it sounds like provide the concrete clues to the level of transfer occurring.

◆ SOMEWHERES ◆

## SITUATIONAL DISPOSITIONS FOR TRANSFER

| Model | Illustration | Transfer Disposition | Looks Like | Sounds Like |
|---|---|---|---|---|
| BIRDS<br>Ollie the Head-in-the-Sand Ostrich | | Overlooks | Persists in writing in manuscript form rather than cursive. (New skill overlooked or avoided.) | "I get it right on the dittos, but I forget to use punctuation when I write an essay." (Not applying mechanical learning.) |
| Dan the Drilling Woodpecker | | Duplicates | Plagiarism is the most obvious student artifact of duplication. (Unable to synthesize in own words.) | "Mine is not to question why—just invert and multiply." [When dividing fractions.] (No understanding of what he or she is doing.) |
| Laura the Look-Alike Penguin | | Replicates | "Bed to Bed" or narrative style. "He got up. He did this. He went to bed." or "He was born. He did this. He died." (Student portfolio of work never varies.) | "Paragraphing means I must have three 'indents' per page." (Tailors into own story or essay, but paragraphs inappropriately.) |
| Jonathan Livingston Seagull | | Integrates | Student writing essay incorporates newly learned French words. (Applying: weaving old and new.) | "I always try to guess (predict) what's going to happen next on T.V. shows." (Connects to prior knowledge and experience; relates what's learned to personal experience.) |
| Cathy the Carrier Pigeon | | Maps | Graphs information for a social studies report with the help of the math teacher to actually design the graphs. (Connecting to another.) | From a parent: "Tina suggested we brainstorm our vacation ideas and rank them to help us decide." (Carries new skills into life situations.) |
| Samantha the Soaring Eagle | | Innovates | After studying flow charts for computer class, student constructs a Rube Goldberg-type invention. (Innovates; diverges; goes beyond and creates novelty.) | "I took the idea of the Mr. Potato Head and created a mix-and-match grid of ideas for our Earth Day project." (Generalizes ideas from experience and transfers creatively.) |

Figure 10 Situational Dispositions for Transfer

◆ S O M E W H E R E S ◆

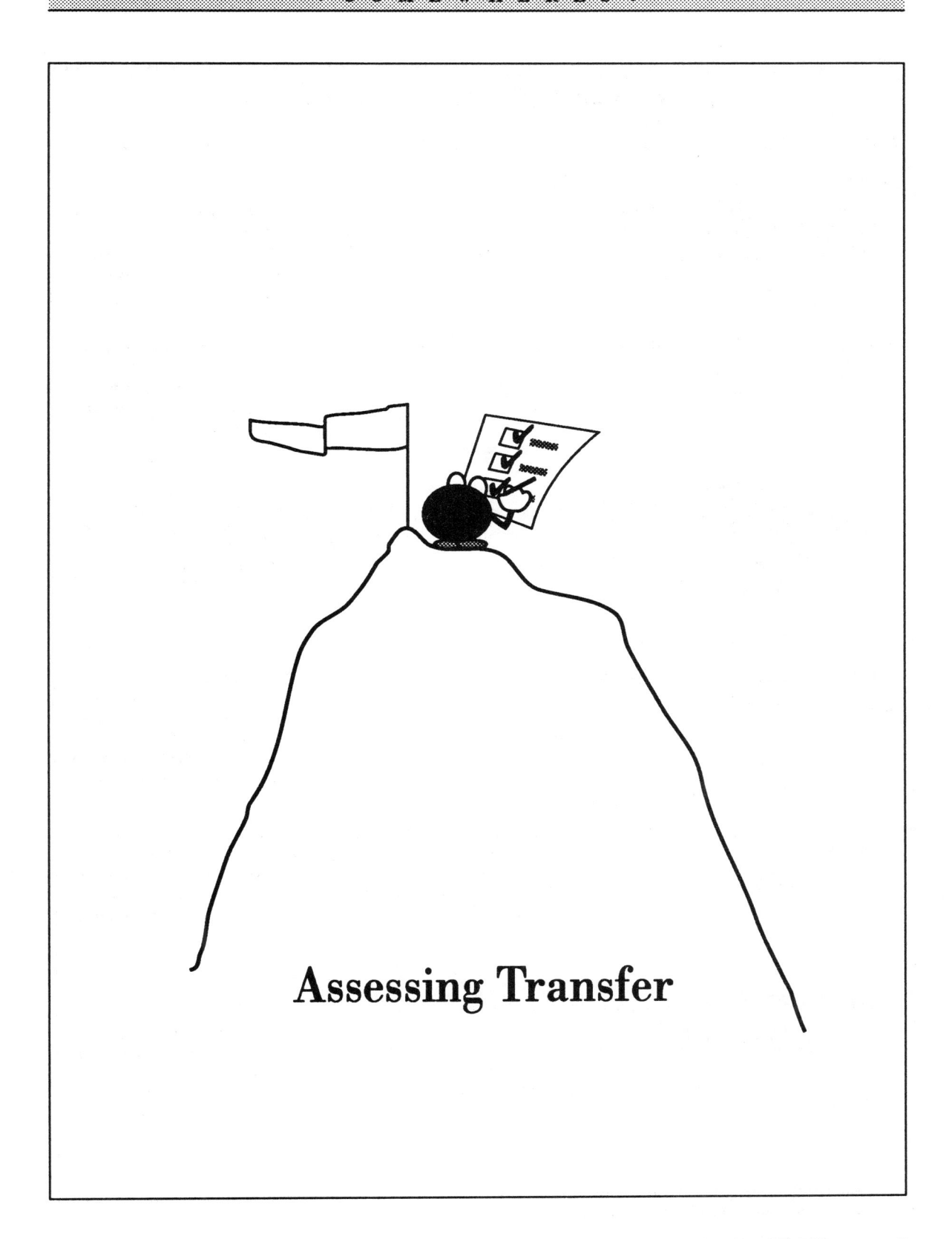

# Assessing Transfer

◆ SOMEWHERES ◆

## ASSESSMENT

**Ollie the Head-in-the-Sand Ostrich**

**Overlooks**

# Overlooking

Ollie the Head-in-the-Sand Ostrich overlooks transfer. This learner misses appropriate opportunities and persists in former ways. This learner may be intentionally or unintentionally overlooking the opportunities for transfer. Sometimes, learners choose not to use something new—for whatever reasons. "The computer takes too long." But, sometimes they unintentionally overlook an opportunity to apply something in a new context because they just don't "get it"; they miss the connection. "Why don't you just multiply the number of words in a line by the number of lines—instead of counting every word?" "Oh? I never thought of that."

### A Sample

Think about a lesson, unit, topic, chapter, or theme. Write what it would sound like or look like for a student to *overlook transfer; intentionally exclude;* or *unintentionally miss* taking the targeted something somewhere—within the content, across disciplines, or into life situations.

*Did you choose not to use _____ because _____?*

Math: Did I choose not to use the SCAMPER problem-solving model because I didn't remember it or because I was more confident with my "old way"?

*Does _____ seem unrelated to _____? Why?*

Science: This unit on genetics seems unrelated to the plant and animal unit. We never talked about hereditary characteristics of plants and animals.

*Are you overlooking something that you should be thinking about?*

Social Studies: In trying to get a focus for my report, am I overlooking some of the cues I've learned about in the research unit?

◆ SOMEWHERES ◆

## ASSESSMENT

# Overlooking

Ollie the Head-in-the-Sand Ostrich overlooks transfer. This learner misses appropriate opportunities and persists in former ways. This learner may be intentionally or unintentionally overlooking the opportunities for transfer. Sometimes, learners choose not to use something new—for whatever reasons. "The computer takes too long." But, sometimes they unintentionally overlook an opportunity to apply something in a new context because they just don't "get it"; they miss the connection. "Why don't you just multiply the number of words in a line by the number of lines—instead of counting every word?" "Oh? I never thought of that."

**Ollie the Head-In-the-Sand Ostrich**

**Overlooks**

## Your Example

Think about a lesson, unit, topic, chapter, or theme. Write what it would sound like or look like for a student to *overlook transfer; intentionally exclude;* or *unintentionally miss* taking the targeted something somewhere—within the content, across disciplines, or into life situations.

*Did you choose not to use _____ because _____?*

*Does _____ seem unrelated to _____? Why?*

*Are you overlooking something that you should be thinking about?*

The Somewheres of Transfer 107

◆ S O M E W H E R E S ◆

## ASSESSMENT

**Dan the Drilling Woodpecker**

**Duplicates**

# Duplicating

Dan the Drilling Woodpecker duplicates in transfer. This learner performs the drill or reproduces the product exactly as practiced. There is no deviation or personalization. The transfer appears quite rehearsed, mechanical, directed, and procedural. ("Divide, multiply, subtract. Bring down." "Divide, multiply, subtract. Bring down.")

Plagiarism is the ultimate example of duplication. "Where can I find that?" "I used the definition verbatim," or "I need a pattern in order to make this," are verbal clues to duplicated transfer.

### A Sample

Think about a lesson, unit, topic, chapter, or theme. Write what it would sound like or look like for a student to *duplicate; copy or reproduce; or use "as is"*—within the content, across disciplines, or into life situations.

*Is there something here that you could have incorporated if you had known?*

Math: I can use the equation for area (A=2l x 2w) to figure out how big a rug I need.

*Is there an idea to "steal" here?*

Social Studies: I'm going to take the report outline from English and use it exactly as it is for my report on Africa.

*What if you borrow _____?*

Language Arts: What if I borrow this idea exactly as it's stated here and quote Emerson to open my speech?

◆ SOMEWHERES ◆

## ASSESSMENT

# Duplicating

Dan the Drilling Woodpecker duplicates in transfer. This learner performs the drill or reproduces the product exactly as practiced. There is no deviation or personalization. The transfer appears quite rehearsed, mechanical, directed, and procedural. ("Divide, multiply, subtract. Bring down." "Divide, multiply, subtract. Bring down.")

Plagiarism is the ultimate example of duplication. "Where can I find that?" "I used the definition verbatim" or "I need a pattern in order to make this" are verbal clues to duplicated transfer.

**Dan the Drilling Woodpecker**

**Duplicates**

### Your Example

Think about a lesson, unit, topic, chapter, or theme. Write what it would sound like or look like for a student to *duplicate; copy or reproduce; or use "as is"*—within the content, across disciplines, or into life situations.

*Is there something here that you could have incorporated if you had known?*




*Is there an idea to "steal" here?*




*What if you borrow _____?*




The Somewheres of Transfer   109

◆ SOMEWHERES ◆

## ASSESSMENT

**Laura the Look-Alike Penguin**

**Replicates**

# Replicating

Laura the Look-Alike Penguin replicates. This learner tailors the learning for personal relevance. Using a given model the learner structures the variables to meet personal needs. ("I used the idea of note cards, but I didn't actually use cards. I just divided the paper into same-size sections so I could do it on my computer.") However, every application (although modified for relevant use) is used in a similar contextual framework. The replicator exemplifies simple transfer and does not break out of the mold she or he establishes.

### A Sample

Think about a lesson, unit, topic, chapter, or theme. Write what it would sound like or look like for a student to *replicate, adapt, tailor, or modify the idea*—within the content, across disciplines, or into life situations.

*Could you change something?*

*Geography: If I change the map from a topographical map to a relief map, the elevation will be more obvious.*

*Next time, what can you do to adapt this idea?*

*Science: Next time I do a lab, I'm going to read the material after the lecture. It makes more sense to me then.*

*What do you need to do to use this in your circumstances or to tailor for your needs?*

*Art: Since I can't draw people very well, I'm going to do caricatures for my poster illustrations.*

## ASSESSMENT

### Replicating

Laura the Look-Alike Penguin replicates. This learner tailors the learning for personal relevance. Using a given model the learner structures the variables to meet personal needs. ("I used the idea of note cards, but I didn't actually use cards. I just divided the paper into same-size sections so I could do it on my computer.") However, every application (although modified for relevant use) is used in a similar contextual framework. The replicator exemplifies simple transfer and does not break out of the mold she or he establishes.

**Laura the Look-Alike Penguin**

**Replicates**

### Your Example

Think about a lesson, unit, topic, chapter, or theme. Write what it would sound like or look like for a student to *replicate, adapt, tailor, or modify the idea*—within the content, across disciplines, or into life situations.

*Could you change something?*

*Next time, what can you do to adapt this idea?*

*What do you need to do to use this in your circumstances or to tailor for your needs?*

The Somewheres of Transfer

◆ SOMEWHERES ◆

## ASSESSMENT

**Jonathan Livingston Seagull**

*Integrates*

# Integrating

Jonathan Livingston Seagull integrates with a raised consciousness. This learner, acutely aware of an idea, combines the new learning with prior knowledge and past experiences. The transfer is subtle and may not always be easy to track because the learning is assimilated so naturally into the learner's existing framework. In fact, sometimes the learner actually says, "I already knew how to outline." or "I've always done my essays from an outline." It's not new—but maybe now explicit, rather than implicit. In this integrated level of complex transfer, the learner folds the new learning in with the old, blending the two together.

### A Sample

Think about a lesson, unit, topic, chapter, or theme. Write what it would sound like or look like for a student to *integrate; combine; assimilate; and weave new ideas into existing ideas*—within the content, across disciplines, or into life situations.

*Does this bring an old idea to mind?*

Technology Lab: Using this DRAW program reminds me of when I was a kid doing Etch A Sketch. I drew a map of the United States with all the states represented.

*How could you combine this with ___?*

Business Education: What I'm learning about budgeting in accounting right now could be combined with my travel lesson for social studies. I could include an expense accounting of the trip.

*How is this like _____ because both _____.*

Literature: <u>The Old Man in the Sea</u> is like <u>Moby Dick</u> because both men persevere and both are passionate in their quest.

112 HOW TO TEACH FOR TRANSFER

◆ SOMEWHERES ◆

## ASSESSMENT

### Integrating

**Jonathan Livingston Seagull**

*Integrates*

Jonathan Livingston Seagull integrates with a raised consciousness. This learner, acutely aware of an idea, combines the new learning with prior knowledge and past experiences. The transfer is subtle and may not always be easy to track because the learning is assimilated so naturally into the learner's existing framework. In fact, sometimes the learner actually says, "I already knew how to outline" or "I've always done my essays from an outline." It's not new—but maybe now explicit, rather than implicit. In this integrated level of complex transfer, the learner folds the new learning in with the old, blending the two together.

### Your Example

Think about a lesson, unit, topic, chapter, or theme. Write what it would sound like or look like for a student to ***integrate; combine; assimilate; and weave new ideas into existing ideas***—within the content, across disciplines, or into life situations.

*Does this bring an old idea to mind?*




*How could you combine this with ___?*




*How is this like ___ because both ___.*

The Somewheres of Transfer   113

◆ S O M E W H E R E S ◆

## ASSESSMENT

**Cathy the Carrier Pigeon**

**Maps**

# Mapping

Cathy the Carrier Pigeon deliberately moves the learning from one context to a different context. This learner makes explicit bridges by strategically planning future applications. The transfer seems crystal clear and application is made with ease. "I'm going to use the science report on pollution in my communications class. We have to develop public service commercial messages."

What distinguishes this transfer from the previous models of integrated use is the explicitness with which the learner applies the ideas. There is obvious intent to move ideas from one context to another in this model and the risk taking required is greater than in the previous levels.

### A Sample

Think about a lesson, unit, topic, chapter, or theme. Write what it would sound like or look like for a student to *map; strategize; plan;* or *anticipate* taking the targeted something somewhere—within the content, across disciplines, or into life situations.

*Can you apply this idea in several ways?*

French: I can use the concepts and techniques of the impressionists both in my sketching and in my painting. It's a new way to represent my idea.

*How might you carry this idea across to _____?*

Social Studies: I think I can use the idea of political cartoons in my English report. They will enhance my written words.

*How will this bridge into _____?*

Literature: I'm going to take this idea of the surprise ending of O. Henry and use it in our skit for the drama class.

114  HOW TO TEACH FOR TRANSFER

◆ S O M E W H E R E S ◆

### ASSESSMENT

# Mapping

**Cathy the Carrier Pigeon**

Cathy the Carrier Pigeon deliberately moves the learning from one context to a different context. This learner makes explicit bridges by strategically planning future applications. The transfer seems crystal clear and application is made with ease. "I'm going to use the science report on pollution in my communications class. We have to develop public service commercial messages."

What distinguishes this transfer from the previous models of integrated use is the explicitness with which the learner applies the ideas. There is obvious intent to move ideas from one context to another in this model and the risk taking required is greater than in the previous levels.

**Maps**

## Your Example

Think about a lesson, unit, topic, chapter, or theme. Write what it would sound like or look like for a student to *map; strategize; plan; or anticipate* taking the targeted something somewhere—within the content, across disciplines, or into life situations.

*Can you apply this idea in several ways?*




*How might you carry this idea across to _____?*




*How will this bridge into _____?*




**The Somewheres of Transfer**

• SOMEWHERES •

## ASSESSMENT

**Samantha the Soaring Eagle**

**Innovates**

# Innovating

Samantha (or Sam) the Soaring Eagle innovates. This student creatively transforms learning by grasping the seeds of an idea and researching, reshaping, reforming, or renaming to such an extent that the original learning may become vastly modified in unique ways. "Rather than write about me and my summer vacation, I wrote about it from the point of view of my dog, Rags. I bet you wondered why I called it 'Dog Days of Summer.'" This level of transfer is noted for its novel ideas and the risk taking that accompanies such creative thinking. Games are wonderful connection makers—anything goes!

### A Sample

Think about a lesson, unit, topic, chapter, or theme. Write what it would sound like or look like for a student to *Innovate; create; reshape; Invent; or transform*—within the content, across disciplines, or into life situations.

*I've totally redesigned....*

Art: I've totally redesigned my portfolio. I took black and white photos of everything and arranged the photos on different colored paper. It presents a cleaner looking album of work.

*A new idea incubating....*

Math: An idea incubating is to use equations in other subject areas than math. For example: plot plus character plus setting equal fiction; or water plus sunlight plus nutrients equal healthy plant; or people plus weapons plus disagreement equal war whereas people minus weapons plus disagreement equal negotiations.

*What if....*

Language Arts: What if I begin at the end and flashback to the beginning in my short story — sort of like they did in <u>Love Story</u>. I think it'll capture the readers attention.

116   HOW TO TEACH FOR TRANSFER

◆ SOMEWHERES ◆

## ASSESSMENT

# Innovating

Samantha (or Sam) the Soaring Eagle innovates. This student creatively transforms learning by grasping the seeds of an idea and researching, reshaping, reforming, or renaming to such an extent that the original learning may become vastly modified in unique ways. "Rather than write about me and my summer vacation, I wrote about it from the point of view of my dog, Rags. I bet you wondered why I called it 'Dog Days of Summer.'" This level of transfer is noted for its novel ideas and the risk taking that accompanies such creative thinking. Games are wonderful connection makers—anything goes!

**Samantha the Soaring Eagle**

*Innovates*

## Your Example

Think about a lesson, unit, topic, chapter, or theme. Write what it would sound like or look like for a student to *Innovate; create; reshape; Invent; or transform*—within the content, across disciplines, or into life situations.

*I've totally redesigned....*

*A new idea incubating...*

*What if....*

The Somewheres of Transfer 117

## CONCLUSION

The six dispositions do not necessarily occur in sequence, but there seems to be a logical hierarchy. The first three reflect simple transfer with minimal risk taking involved, while the last three models involve more complexity, and the last two require considerable mindfulness and risk taking.

When the teacher and the student become aware of the transfer levels, the likelihood that transfer will occur is increased. In other words, once you know about the levels and their symptoms, you can't *not* know! The awareness is there. The level of transfer starts to be consciously monitored. Interestingly, this self-awareness seems to be accompanied by a sense of responsibility, also. Once aware of transfer, students feel more accountable to transfer and are more likely to use new ideas. In addition, once teachers and students put their radars out for evidence of transfer, transfer gets more attention. As teachers and students become tuned in to the symptoms, transfer from one level to the next can be readily facilitated. For instance, questions, self-initiated by the student or posed by a peer or mentor, can move transfer along.

To transfer this idea of transfer, Figure 11 suggests possible approaches to redesigning, designing, or refining lessons. By looking at previous lessons or upcoming lessons through the fresh window of transfer, teachers can set new curricular priorities. In addition, once we identify the priority *somethings,* teachers can target the specific similarities for transfer within the content, across disciplines, or into life situations. And, to achieve the desired outcomes of taking those important *somethings* to the specified *somewheres,* teachers can select the various *somehows* of hugging and bridging strategies or combinations thereof to insure transfer of learning.

In closing, **there are *somethings* that we want to *somehow* transfer *somewhere*.** Hopefully, this discussion will provide the catalyst for us to begin the work of teaching for transfer not for a test, but for a lifetime.

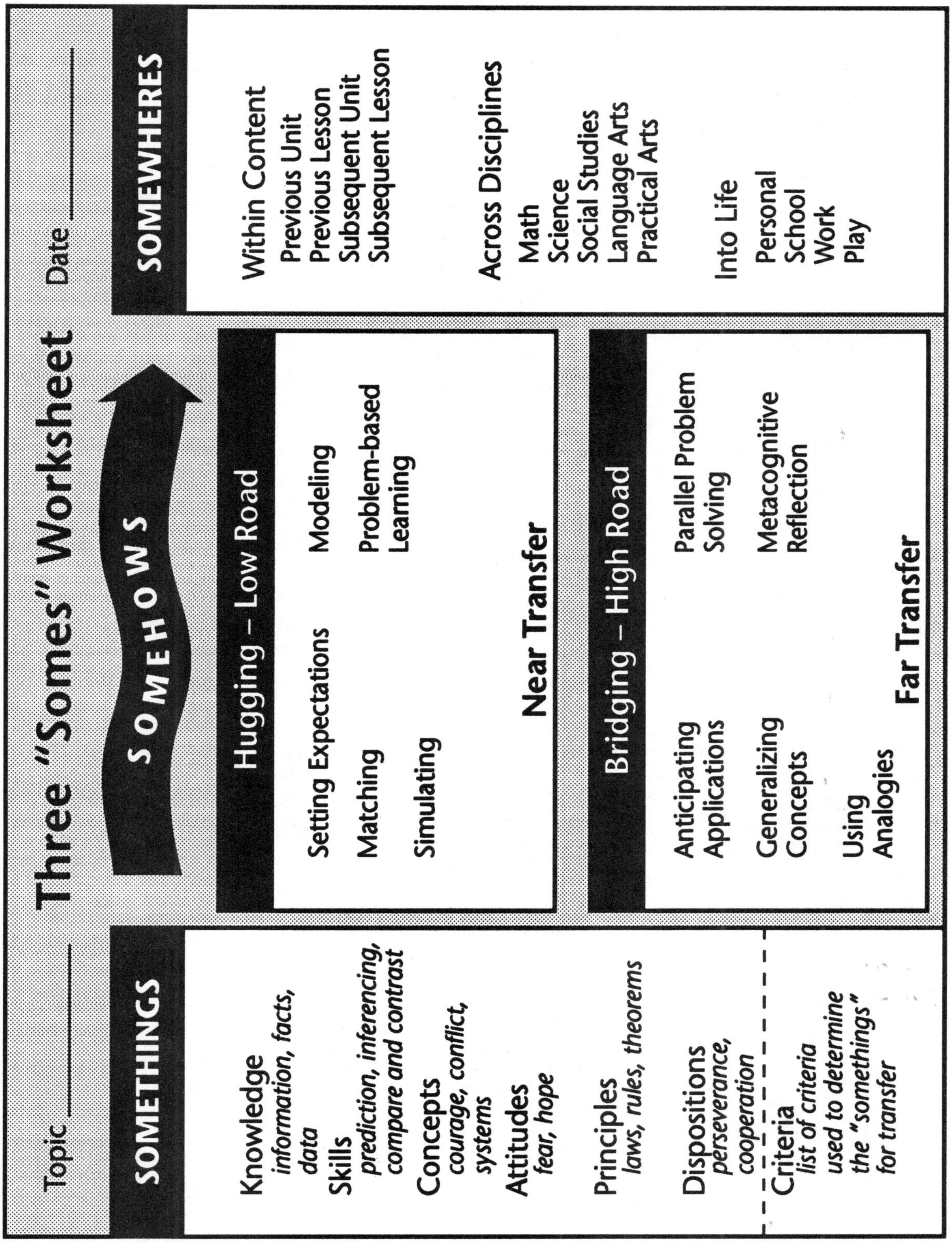

◆ SOMEWHERES ◆

## Three "Somes" Worksheet

Topic _____  Date _____

**SOMETHINGS**

**Knowledge**
*information, facts, data*
**Skills**
*prediction, inferencing, compare and contrast*
**Concepts**
*courage, conflict, systems*
**Attitudes**
*fear, hope*
**Principles**
*laws, rules, theorems*
**Dispositions**
*perseverance, cooperation*
- - - - - -
**Criteria**
*list of criteria used to determine the "somethings" for transfer*

**SOMEHOWS**

**Hugging – Low Road**

Setting Expectations    Modeling
Matching                Problem-based
Simulating              Learning

**Near Transfer**

**Bridging – High Road**

Anticipating            Parallel Problem
Applications            Solving
Generalizing            Metacognitive
Concepts                Reflection
Using
Analogies

**Far Transfer**

**SOMEWHERES**

**Within Content**
Previous Unit
Previous Lesson
Subsequent Unit
Subsequent Lesson

**Across Disciplines**
Math
Science
Social Studies
Language Arts
Practical Arts

**Into Life**
Personal
School
Work
Play

**Figure 11 Sample Three "Somes" Worksheet**

The Somewheres of Transfer   119

# Glossary

**ANTICIPATING APPLICATIONS (BRIDGING STRATEGY)** In this strategy, the teacher asks students to brainstorm where else some knowledge or strategy they have been studying might be used. Or the teacher may suggest several areas of application outside the current focus and provide brief practice with them. Thus, applications of the knowledge or strategy to the other contexts are anticipated rather than left to spontaneous transfer.

For example, a history teacher might introduce concept mapping to help students represent causal patterns in historical events. After the students gain some familiarity with the technique, the teacher might ask them to brainstorm possible applications of concept mapping to other subject matters—diagramming stories in English or concepts in mathematics, for instance.

**BO PEEP THEORY OF TRANSFER: *TRANSFER TAKES CARE OF ITSELF*** The tacit theory of transfer behind most educational practice is that transfer takes care of itself: students learn knowledge and skills in one context and automatically transfer what they learn to other appropriate contexts. One might call this the "Bo Peep" theory, because it treats transfer the way Bo Peep treated her sheep: "Leave them alone, and they'll come home, wagging their tails behind them." Unfortunately, research shows that the Bo Peep theory is generally mistaken. Transfer does not occur without special attention. (See "Lost Sheep theory" and "Good Shepherd theory").

**CRITERIA FOR WHAT TO TEACH FOR TRANSFER** Teaching for transfer involves selecting *something* to be transferred—certain knowledge, concepts, skills, or whatever. This, in turn, calls for thoughtful consideration of what elements of the curriculum are worth teaching for transfer (not to mention worth teaching at all!). What makes a topic worthwhile as a candidate for transfer is, of course, its potential significance in other areas. In appraising a topic's potential, one can check the following three areas:

- *Significance within the disciplines*—does the topic have broad significance within its own and perhaps other disciplines?
- *Societal significance*—does the topic speak to problems and concerns of society at large?
- *Student needs/interests/aspirations*—does the topic resonate with students' hopes, desires, curiosities, needs, and so on?

**FAR TRANSFER** A rough distinction is drawn between "near transfer" (see) and "far transfer." Far transfer refers to transfer between contexts that are very different. Here are some examples of far transfer:

- Using problem-solving skills acquired in mathematics to puzzle out an exercise in English.
- Using knowledge of history to understand current events unfolding in the daily paper.
- Using knowledge from literature to think about one's own life situations.

Of course, the distinction between near and far transfer is only a rough one and there are many intermediate cases.

**GENERALIZING CONCEPTS (BRIDGING STRATEGY)** In this strategy, the teacher scaffolds a discussion beginning with a particular topic, leading students to generalize from it in far-reaching ways. For example, working from a short story that students have read, the teacher might call for generalizations about human nature, and examples of those generalizations from other stories and everyday experience.

**GOOD SHEPHERD THEORY OF TRANSFER: *TRANSFER WILL HAPPEN WITH SHEPHERDING*** Both research and classroom experience argue that we can obtain considerable near and far transfer if we teach in ways that foster transfer. Such teaching might be called "shepherding transfer," because teachers act as guides and prompters to "shepherd" knowledge and skills from one context to another.

**HIGH ROAD TRANSFER** High road transfer is one of two fundamental mechanisms of transfer identified by Gavriel Salomon and David Perkins. High road transfer occurs through *mindful abstraction* of knowledge or skills from one context and *mindful application* in another context. It is a thoughtful, effort-demanding process, intellectual in character.

High road transfer is particularly important as a way of achieving far transfer, because the mechanisms of low road transfer do not readily bridge large gaps (*see* "Low road transfer").

- A student abstracts some diagramming strategies from mathematics studies for representing problems; the student applies these diagramming strategies in English to understand the structure of a story.
- A student notices how two siblings in a novel treat one another, sometimes getting along, sometimes not getting along; the student becomes more mindful about interactions at home with a sibling, improving the relationship.
- A student learns about the principle of entropy in physics. The student abstracts the general idea that random events tend to lead to an accumulation of haphazardness, and recognizes that entropy is at work in making his or her desk and class notes messy.

Of course, learning situations can easily mix low road and high road transfer. Both mechanisms can operate at once.

**INERT KNOWLEDGE** Considerable research shows that a startling amount of the knowledge that people acquire in subject matter instruction is "inert." This means that the knowledge is "there" in memory for the multiple-choice quiz. But the knowledge is passive. It is not retrieved in contexts of active problem solving or creativity, such as writing an essay. So inert knowledge does not really contribute much to the cognitive ability of the learner except for performance on school quizzes. One of the goals of teaching transfer is teaching for active rather than inert knowledge.

**KWL CHART** This is a graphic organizer that helps in assessing prior knowledge and current questions for a learning task, and then helps assess what was actually learned after the task is completed. It is a triple T-Chart with the headings, "What We **K**now," "What We **W**ant to Find Out," "What We **L**earned."

**LOST SHEEP THEORY OF TRANSFER: *TRANSFER DOESN'T HAPPEN*** Discouraged by the track record of spontaneous transfer, some theorists have concluded that people simply do not transfer very well, especially for "far transfer" (see). Knowledge and skills acquired in one context do not apply very well to other contexts. By and large, learners have to learn anew in each distinctive context. However, considerable research shows that this theory is mistaken. Under the right conditions, learners transfer a lot. (*See* "Bo Peep theory" and "Good Shepherd theory.")

**LOW ROAD TRANSFER** Low road transfer is one of two fundamental mechanisms of transfer identified by Gavriel Salomon and David Perkins. Low road transfer occurs by the *automatic triggering* of well-learned knowledge or skills by perceptually similar situations. It is not a very thoughtful, intellectual process, but more of a spontaneous, reflexive one. It is thus more efficient than high road transfer, but as a trend yields near transfer much more than far transfer.

Low road transfer can reach somewhat further over time, because knowledge and skill can gradually spread from one context to a similar one, to another similar one, and so on. Thus, low road transfer is facilitated by practicing knowledge and skill in a variety of similar contexts, thus "spreading out" the knowledge or skill in question over them.

## ◆ GLOSSARY ◆

Here are some examples of low road transfer:

- A student learns basic arithmetic skills in arithmetic; these are automatically evoked when an arithmetic problem arises in science.
- Students learn a problem-solving strategy for one kind of arithmetic problem. The teacher immediately gives a somewhat different kind of problem, but with some similarity. Students carry over the strategy to the new kind of problem, thus "spreading" its utility more widely.
- The English teacher teaches some basic reading strategies, giving students practice in several different kinds of reading to "spread" the habit across multiple genres.

Of course, learning situations can easily mix low road and high road transfer. Both mechanisms can operate at once.

**MATCHING (HUGGING STRATEGY)** Matching simply means making the instructional experience just the same as the desired transfer outcome. You engage students in the very performances you are trying to develop, so there is no gap left between the instructional experience and the performance.

For example, if we want students to take a stand, advocate a position, and support it with detail, we need to engage them in doing just that, for instance through class or small group debates. If we want students to learn how history speaks to contemporary events, we should engage them in thinking about exactly that.

**METACOGNITION** Metacognition is a technical term that means "thinking about thinking"—your own, or someone else's, or thinking about thinking in general. Most typically, what is meant is thinking about your own thinking.

There are many aspects to thinking that one can fruitfully think about—for example, how one solves problems, how one remembers and memorizes (sometimes called "metamemory"), how one monitors one's attention and keeps oneself on track (sometimes called "attention monitoring").

Metacognition is a mental activity important to high road transfer. Research shows that people who are aware of their own thinking and reflect upon it are more likely to achieve transfer by way of the high road.

**MODELING (HUGGING STRATEGY)** Modeling means demonstrating the desired behavior while giving a running metacognitive monologue (or followed by a metacognitive discussion) cuing the key elements. In other words, the teacher shows and labels a model of the behavior the students are to adopt. For example, demonstrating a "pre-reading" strategy, a teacher might read aloud the headings and captions of an article, speculate aloud as to what they suggested about the whole article, and generate some questions to ask aloud while reading the article fully.

**NEAR TRANSFER** A rough distinction is drawn between "near transfer" and "far transfer" (see). Near transfer refers to transfer between contexts that are quite similar. Here are some examples of near transfer:

- Using a problem-solving skill you acquired in math for another kind of problem in math.
- Using a piece of historical knowledge in thinking about another episode in history, making a comparison.
- Using driving skills for driving a car for driving a small truck.

Of course, the distinction between near and far transfer is only a rough one and there are many intermediate cases.

**PARALLEL PROBLEM SOLVING (BRIDGING STRATEGY)** In this bridging strategy, students solve problems with parallel structure and content in two different areas. The students gain an appreciation for the similarities and contrasts between the areas, along with a better sense of the problem-solving processes themselves. Often, although not necessarily, one of the areas concerns personal or everyday life. For example, students from an inner city area might reason about the causes of gang warfare. Then, in similar manner, reason about the causes of international rivalry and war.

**PROBLEM-BASED LEARNING (HUGGING STRATEGY)** Problem-based learning means engaging students in learning a body of facts, ideas, and/or procedures through active, open-ended problem solving. The name "problem-based learning" suggests a goal of improving problem-solving skills, and problem-based learning may do so. But this is not its principal goal! Instead, the aim is to develop *active* rather than *inert* knowledge, that is, knowledge likely to be retrieved in open-ended problem-solving situations in the future. Problem-based learning is a hugging strategy because its philosophy is, "If you want active use of knowledge later, build active use of knowledge into the learning process."

SCAFFOLDING Scaffolding is an established technical term for a pattern of interaction between learners and a teacher, parent, or other person in a teaching role. In scaffolding, the teacher neither leaves the learners alone nor provides "how to" information (although the teacher may provide some information to kick things off). Rather, the teacher interacts with the learners, offering leading questions, hints, and prompts to help the learners along. These questions, hints, and prompts are the "scaffold" that allows the learners to work through the problem at hand as much on their own as possible.

The art of scaffolding is a balancing act. The teacher scaffolds as little as possible, but enough to keep up the pace of the activity. The teacher reduces the scaffolding as the learners gain knowledge and confidence.

SETTING EXPECTATIONS (HUGGING STRATEGY) At the beginning of a piece of instruction, teachers can alert students to the expectation that the students will find what they learn useful in other related situations. Teachers can encourage students to anticipate using what they learn and try to be alert and flexible in seeking opportunities to do so.

For example, teaching a reading skill in English class, the teacher can alert students to the idea that this skill can also be used for similar kinds of reading later in the term, or in history class.

SIMULATING (HUGGING STRATEGY) Simulating is like "matching" (see), but serves in situations where it is impossible, inconvenient, or imprudent to replicate the actual situation to which you want transfer. Instead, therefore, you simulate it. Students experience an approximation in actions and feelings of the actual situation by means of the simulation. For example, students might role-play the trial of the Big Bad Wolf of "The Three Little Pigs" to learn about bias and jury selection. Students might undergo mock job interviews to prepare for real ones.

SOMETHING, SOMEHOW, SOMEWHERE This is a shorthand reminder for three things to think about when you are planning to teach for transfer. In a sentence, you are going to transfer some*thing* (some skill, knowledge, strategy, etc.) to some*where* (some other context of application—a different subject matter, everyday life, etc.). And, to do that, you have to do it some*how*. You have to utilize one or more strategies of hugging or bridging.

In summary, you can organize your planning of teaching for transfer by asking yourself:

- What are the some*things* (knowledge, skills, strategies, etc.) I want to transfer?
- What are the some*hows* (hugging and bridging strategies) I'm going to use to promote transfer?
- What are the some*wheres* (other subject matters, everyday life) I want to transfer to?

TRANSFER "Transfer of learning" simply means the use in a new context of knowledge and skills acquired in an earlier context. The knowledge or skills transferred can be very specific—a fact about history or grammar. Or they can be very general—a theory, a principle, a thinking skill.

USING ANALOGIES (BRIDGING STRATEGY) The teacher poses (or draws from the students) a potential analogy between two very different areas and scaffolds the students in "unpacking" the analogy—elaborating on it and exploring how well it holds up, examining the similarities and differences.

For example, a teacher might invite comparisons between the atom and the solar system: In what ways are they analogous, in what ways dissimilar? In the same spirit, a teacher might invite comparisons between the family and the government of a state or nation.

# Bibliography

Bartlett, P. *Review of Education Research*, Vol. 60, No. 4, p. 206. Winter, 1990.

Bellanca, J. and Fogarty, R. *Blueprints for Thinking in the Cooperative Classroom.* Palatine, IL: Skylight Publishing, 1990.

Beyer, B. *Practical Strategies for the Teaching of Thinking.* Boston: Allyn and Bacon, 1987.

Brandt, R. "On Teaching Thinking: A Conversation with Arthur Costa." *Educational Leadership.* Vol. 45, No. 7, p. 11, April 1988.

Costa, A. "Orchestrating the Second Wave." *Cogitare*, Vol. 5, No. 2, 1991a.

Costa, A. "The Search for Intelligent Life." *The School As A Home For The Mind.* Palatine, IL: Skylight Publishing, 1991b.

Costa, A., Bellanca, J., and Fogarty, R. (Eds.). *If Minds Matter: A Foreword to the Future.* Palatine, IL: Skylight Publishing, 1992.

Costa, A. and Garmston, R. "The Art of Cognitive Coaching: Supervision for Intelligent Teaching." Paper presented at the Annual Conference of the Association for Supervision and Curriculum Development, Chicago, March 1985.

Cousins, N. *Human Options.* New York: Norton, 1981.

Eisner, E. PDK/IRI Critical Issues Seminar: Rosemont, IL, February, 1991.

Feuerstein, R. *Instrumental Enrichment.* Baltimore: University Park Press, 1980.

Fogarty, R. *From Training to Transfer: The Role of Creativity in the Adult Learner.* Doctoral Dissertation, Loyola University of Chicago, 1989.

Fogarty, R. *The Mindful School: How To Integrate The Curricula.* Palatine, IL: Skylight Publishing, 1991.

Fogarty, R. and Bellanca, J. *Patterns For Thinking: Patterns For Transfer.* Palatine, IL: Skylight Publishing, 1989.

Fullan, M. *The Meaning of Educational Change.* New York: Teachers College Press, 1982.

Hord, S. and Loucks, S. *A Concerns-Based Model for Delivery of Inservice.* CBFM Project - Research and Development Center for Teacher Education, The University of Texas at Austin.

Hunter, M. *Teach for Transfer.* El Segundo, CA: TIP Publications, 1982.

Joyce, B. *Improving America's Schools.* New York: Longman, 1986.

Joyce, B. and Showers, B. "Improving Inservice Training: The Message of Research." *Educational Leadership.* Vol. 43, No. 8, p. 380, February 1980.

Joyce, B. and Showers, B. *Power in Staff Development Through Research and Training.* Alexandria, VA: ASCD, 1983.

# ◆ BIBLIOGRAPHY ◆

Marzano, R. and Arredondo, D. "Restructuring Schools Through the Teaching of Thinking Skills." *Educational Leadership.* Vol. 43, No. 8, p. 23, May 1986.

Parnes, S. *Aha! Insights Into Creative Behavior.* Buffalo: D.O.K, 1975.

Perkins, D. "Thinking Frames." Paper delivered at ASCD Conference on Approaches to Teaching Thinking, Alexandria, VA, p. 14-15, August 6, 1988.

Perkins, D. *Knowledge As Design.* Hillsdale, NJ: Erlbaum, p. 222-231, 1986.

Perkins, D.; Barell, J.; and Fogarty, R. *Teaching For Transfer* (Course Notebook). Palatine, IL: Skylight Publishing, 1989.

Perkins, D. and Salomon, G. "Are Cognitive Skills Context Bound?" *Educational Researcher.* p. 16-25, January-February 1989.

Perkins, D. and Salomon, G. "Teaching For Transfer." *Educational Leadership.* Vol. 46, No. 1, p. 22-32, September 1988.

Polya, G. *How To Solve It.* Princeton, NJ: Doubleday, 1957.

Posner, M. and Keele, S. "Skill Learning." In R. Travers, ed., *Second Handbook of Research on Teaching.* p. 805-831. Chicago: Rand McNally, 1973.

Salomon, G., & Perkins, D. N. Rocky roads to transfer: Rethinking mechanisms of a neglected phenomenon. *Educational Psychologist,* Vol. 24, No. 2, p. 113-142, 1989.

Sergiovanni, T. "Will We Ever Have a True Profession?" *Educational Leadership.* Vol. 44, No. 8, p. 44-49, May 1987.

Sternberg, R. "How Can We Teach Intelligence?" *Educational Leadership.* Vol. 42, No. 1, p. 38-48, September 1984.

Sternberg, R. *Intelligence Applied: Understanding and Increasing Your Intellectual Skills.* New York: Harcourt Brace Jovanovich, 1986.

Tyler, R. "The First Most Significant Curriculum Events In The Twentieth Century." *Educational Leadership.* Vol. 44, No. 4, p. 36-37, December, 1986 - January 1987.

Wittrock, M. "Replacement and Nonreplacement Strategies in Children's Problem Solving." *Journal of Educational Psychology.* Vol. 58, No. 2, p. 69-74, 1967.

There are
one-story intellects,
two-story intellects, and three-story
intellects with skylights. All fact collectors who have
no aim beyond their facts are one-story men. Two-story men compare,
reason, generalize, using the labor of fact collectors as their own.
Three-story men idealize, imagine, predict—
their best illumination comes
from above the skylight.
—*Oliver Wendell*
*Holmes*

**SKYLIGHT PUBLISHING, INC.**